D1035391

Optimum
Social Welfare
and Productivity

THE CHARLES C. MOSKOWITZ LECTURES   NUMBER XIII

Jan Tinbergen

PROFESSOR OF DEVELOPMENT PLANNING
NETHERLANDS SCHOOL OF ECONOMICS

Abram Bergson

GEORGE F. BAKER PROFESSOR OF ECONOMICS
HARVARD UNIVERSITY

Fritz Machlup

PROFESSOR OF ECONOMICS
NEW YORK UNIVERSITY

Oskar Morgenstern

PROFESSOR OF ECONOMICS
NEW YORK UNIVERSITY

HB
99.3
.07

Optimum
Social Welfare
and Productivity

A Comparative View

THE CHARLES C. MOSKOWITZ LECTURES
SCHOOL OF COMMERCE
NEW YORK UNIVERSITY

NEW YORK   NEW YORK UNIVERSITY PRESS   1972

WITHDRAWN

245857

Copyright © 1972 by New York University
Library of Congress Catalog Card
Number: 72-94083

SBN: 8147-8155-1
Manufactured in the United States of America

FOREWORD

The Charles C. Moskowitz Lectures are arranged by the College of Business and Public Administration of New York University and aim at advancing public understanding of the issues that are of major concern to business and the nation. Established through the generosity of Mr. Charles C. Moskowitz, a distinguished alumnus of the College and formerly Vice President-Treasurer and a Director of Loew's, Inc., they have enabled the College to make a significant contribution to public discussion and understanding of important issues facing the American economy and its business enterprises.

The thirteenth in the series of Charles C. Moskowitz Lectures centered on the topic "The Outlook for the Major Competing Economic Systems." This topic seemed especially appropriate at a moment when the President of the United States was engaged in travels to China and to the Soviet Union in pursuit of greater understanding and hopefully of détente. Anticipating continued relaxation among the major powers of the world, we invited four world-famous economists to use the forum provided by the Moskowitz Lectures to discuss the topic. Employing our usual format, we asked Professor Jan Tinbergen of the Netherlands School of Economics, Rotterdam, and first Nobel Laureate in Economics, and Professor Abram Bergson, George F. Baker Professor of Economics at Harvard University, to present papers on facets of the central topic. Thus, Professor Tinbergen spoke about "Some Features of the Optimum Regime," and Professor Bergson presented a paper on "Productivity Under Two Systems: The USSR Versus the West." Comments on these papers were then made by Professors Fritz Machlup and Oskar Morgenstern, both formerly of Princeton University and now at New York University. Professor Machlup organized his comments around the title "The Best Society: Efficiency and Equality," while Professor Morgenstern used the title "Social Aspirations and Optimality."

In his paper Professor Tinbergen addressed this question: What system of economic institutions would produce optimum social welfare? The question is as important as it is complex and difficult, but Professor Tinbergen observed that it is imperative to the future well-being of mankind that it be addressed. One of the fundamental difficulties has to do with the definition of optimum welfare, and, in this connection, he considered the psychological state of mind of the human beings comprising society. In effect, Professor Tinbergen sought a system which would achieve the highest average psychological sense of well-being in society. He expressed the opinion that, while it is presently beyond our capacity to measure accurately such things as "the sense of well-being," in the future, perhaps twenty or thirty years ahead, it would be possible to do so. He thought that, along with some knowledge of the "sense of well-being" of the individuals comprising society, it would be possible to effect, through such means as lump-sum taxes, income transfer arrangements which would simultaneously raise the average welfare of society and avoid undue inhibition of incentives to work and to creativity.

Professor Bergson attempted to make a comparative analysis of productive efficiencies in several Western (capitalistic) economies and the Soviet Union, hoping thereby to discover whether or not such differences as emerged could be traced to variation in the several nations' socioeconomic institutions. His conclusion was that the Soviet Union's record is not so bad as its most vigorous detractors would have us believe, and

the records of the several "capitalistic" nations
are not so good as their protagonists would have
us believe. However, it does appear that the latter, in particular the United States, have a con-
tinuing and significant edge in comparative
productive efficiency.

Professors Machlup and Morgenstern de-
voted the major portion of their comments to
Professor Tinbergen's paper, finding its emphasis
on optimization of social welfare and of transfer
of payments as a means of effecting such optimization especially intriguing and challenging.
They mounted a vigorous challenge to Professor
Tinbergen's theme, concentrating their attention
mainly on the difficulties of defining and measuring social welfare, as well as on the unlikelihood
that profound redistribution of income could be
effected without producing fundamentally adverse effects on work incentives and creativity. In
effect, Professors Machlup and Morgenstern
seemed to have a view of human nature and its
future development which was substantially different from that of Professor Tinbergen. But these
divergencies of perception and of opinion made
the thirteenth in the series of Charles C. Moskowitz Lectures one of the most vigorous and most
stimulating of this exceptional series.

I would be remiss if I closed without adding
a word of appreciation for the always competent
help of Mrs. Patricia Matthias, my Administrative

Assistant. She carried the major burdens in connection with the lecture arrangements and the editorial preparation of this volume. In the last connection, the staff of the New York University Press was also most helpful.

Abraham L. Gitlow

Dean

College of Business and
    Public Administration

New York University

June, 1972

THE CHARLES C. MOSKOWITZ LECTURES were established through the generosity of a distinguished alumnus of the School of Commerce, Mr. Charles C. Moskowitz of the Class of 1914, who retired after many years as Vice President-Treasurer and a Director of Loew's, Inc.

In establishing these lectures, it was Mr. Moskowitz's aim to contribute to the understanding of the function of business and its underlying disciplines in society by providing a public forum for the dissemination of enlightened business theories and practices.

The School of Commerce and New York University are deeply grateful to Mr. Moskowitz for his continued interest in, and contribution to, the educational and public service program of his alma mater.

This volume is the eleventh in the Moskowitz series. The earlier ones were:

February, 1961   *Business Survival in the Sixties*
Thomas F. Patton, President and Chief Executive Officer
Republic Steel Corporation

November, 1961 *The Challenges Facing Management*
Don G. Mitchell, President
General Telephone and Electronics Corporation

November, 1962 *Competitive Private Enterprise Under Government Regulation*
Malcolm A. MacIntyre, President
Eastern Air Lines

November, 1963 *The Common Market: Friend or Competitor?*
Jesse W. Markham, Professor of Economics, Princeton University
Charles E. Fiero, Vice President, The Chase Manhattan Bank
Howard S. Piquet, Senior Specialist in International Economics, Legislative Reference Service, The Library of Congress

November, 1964 *The Forces Influencing the American Economy*
Jules Backman, Research Professor of Economics, New York University

Martin R. Gainsbrugh, Chief Economist and Vice President, National Industrial Conference Board

November, 1965 *The American Market of the Future*
Arno H. Johnson, Vice President and Senior Economist, J. Walter Thompson Company
Gilbert E. Jones, President, IBM World Trade Corporation
Darrell B. Lucas, Professor of Marketing and Chairman of the Department, New York University

November, 1966 *Government Wage-Price Guideposts in the American Economy*
George Meany, President, American Federation of Labor and Congress of Industrial Organizations
Roger M. Blough, Chairman of the Board and Chief Executive Officer, United States Steel Corporation
Neil H. Jacoby, Dean, Graduate School of Business Administration, University of California at Los Angeles

November, 1967 *The Defense Sector in the American Economy*

Jacob K. Javits, United States Senator, New York

Charles J. Hitch, President, University of California

Arthur F. Burns, Chairman, Federal Reserve Board

November, 1968 *The Urban Environment: How It Can Be Improved*

William E. Zisch, Vice-chairman of the Board, Aerojet-General Corporation

Paul H. Douglas, Chairman, National Commission on Urban Problems

Professor of Economics, New School for Social Research

Robert C. Weaver, President, Bernard M. Baruch College of the City University of New York

Former Secretary of Housing and Urban Development

November, 1969 *Inflation: The Problems It Creates and the Policies It Requires*

Arthur M. Okun, Senior Fellow, The Brookings Institution

Henry H. Fowler, General Partner, Goldman, Sachs & Co.

Milton Gilbert, Economic Adviser, Bank for International Settlements

March, 1971   *The Economics of Pollution*
Kenneth E. Boulding, Professor of Economics, University of Colorado
Elvis J. Stahr, President, National Audubon Society
Solomon Fabricant, Professor of Economics, New York University
Former Director, National Bureau of Economic Research
Martin R. Gainsbrugh, Adjunct Professor of Economics, New York University
Chief Economist, National Industrial Conference Board

April, 1971   *Young America in the NOW World*
Hubert H. Humphrey, Senator from Minnesota
Former Vice President of the United States

CONTENTS

SOME FEATURES OF
THE OPTIMUM REGIME

Jan Tinbergen

1. Aim of Lecture

Before tackling the subject of my lecture as announced in its title I want to tell you in a few sentences what I am after. As social scientists I and my colleagues in this field observe, first of all, that every social system is in movement; it changes all the time. We also observe that some countries, the Soviet Union, China or Yugoslavia for example, have social systems different from that of the United States. Even several Western European countries have systems somewhat different from that of the United States. Social scientists are asking themselves continually, and are also asked by their fellow citizens, whether their own system is the best or not, and if not, what

23

changes do they propose. Opinions on this question diverge widely and a considerable number of politicians have rather doctrinaire views. Some schools of thought have expressed their opinion, or rather belief, in such a way that they contribute to an increasing polarization: the creation of two opposite camps, usually with a stamp on them, such as socialism or capitalism. Both as a citizen and as a social scientist I dislike this tendency, and I think it is an increasing danger. Every year we see how social conflicts can easily develop into international conflicts and we all know that with the present type of arms things may easily run out of hand. I am therefore in favor of depolarization, and science generally has the task to draw questions out of the sphere of emotions and shift part of our answer to the realm of objective observation and reasoning. Part only, since we know that not all questions are susceptible to objective treatment. Wherever we succeed in shifting the frontier between belief and science, we have made progress. It helps to solve part of the problem at stake and in doing so bring people closer together instead of making them worse enemies.

My arguments will direct themselves to various groups of our planet; those in Western countries who search for improvement of our societies; those in communist-ruled countries, even if such an attempt were judged futile; those in developing countries who want to let their societies evolve. The problem of finding the best social order has already become more urgent than it was, now that Professors Forrester and Meadows of M.I.T. have faced us with some formidable challenges [2, 6]. If indeed the limits set to human welfare are so much closer than we thought five or ten years ago, the problem of social structure has got a gigantic new relevance.

2. An Interdisciplinary Approach Needed

The task to describe or at least to give a rough sketch of the best social order clearly requires an interdisciplinary approach. This has been understood by such different students of the future as, on the one hand, Kahn and Wiener [3] and, on the other hand, the two MIT colleagues already mentioned; and both groups consist of more than two people. The work done by the scientists mentioned shows already a clear inter-disciplinary nature; they contain, along with those of the other physical sciences, elements of a phys-ical, a chemical, and a biological character, and, in addition, elements of many human sci-ences. Having worked mainly in the field of eco-nomics, and having only some very limited knowl-edge of a few other subjects, I want to defend the thesis that the general framework in which the topic should be treated is the one of welfare economics, although in a way different from traditional welfare economics which has remained too abstract. Welfare economics is the chapter of economics dealing with the question concerning what conditions must be fulfilled in order that social welfare be a maximum, subject to the restrictions within which human society has to live. The definition of social welfare is correctly supposed to be given to the economist and to contain at least one basic ethical element. The restrictions are often specified as the resources available and the production technologies known; at present we would certainly add the technologies of education as an important further element. This brief indication of the welfare economic approach already shows how many other fields of thinking are involved. I am going to point out, later, that some questions involving methodology also pertain. Before elaborating on this I want to repeat what I said on many previous occasions [10, 11], namely, that, to my taste, several economists have formulated in too narrow a way what are the unknowns of the central problem of welfare economics. Often they leave the impression that all we want to learn from the solution is how much work we must do and how much consumption and investment, and at what prices all goods and services will be sold. In other words, the unknowns are a number of economic variables or entities and that is all. In my opinion the problem is much deeper, and the real unknowns of it are the set of institutions (or the several alternative sets of institutions) which by their operation will bring us that optimal situation or, rather, optimal development over time. To put it in somewhat more learned terms: We have to search for a group of institutions the activities of which can be described by a number of equations. The total of these behavior equations of the group should be identical with the conditions for optimal welfare.

The main difference in the approach I take and that which my colleagues in economics take in elaborating the solution to the central problem consists in the time order in which, during our analysis, the contributions from the other disciplines should be taken. While it has been customary for welfare economists to ignore the ethical factors as long as possible and only to consider it after the economic analysis had been finished, I prefer to discuss the social welfare function in the beginning, implying that an ethical choice is made at the beginning. This enormously simplifies the ensuing economic analysis, which in traditional welfare economics has to carry with it the large number of ethical possibilities during the whole process. What I intend to say will become clearer, I hope, during the elaboration of my analysis.

3. A Survey of Possible Approaches

The elaboration of my analysis first requires, I am afraid, a survey of the possible approaches in the form of a systematic presentation and grouping. Since, as we saw, the problem of finding the characteristics of the social welfare optimum, starts with the definition of the social welfare function and the restrictions under which we live, it is only logical to subdivide our system first of all into two categories of approach: (I) the choice of the social welfare function and (II) the choice of the restrictions. Let me warn at once that part of our social aims may also be given the form of restrictions.

By the social welfare function we understand a description of the preference system of the community, consciously or unconsciously, adhered to by the policy makers. For short-term decisions the policy makers will be, as a rule, the *government* administration; for longer-term decisions the legislature, PARLIAMENT and for still longer-term decisions the *political parties*. The preference system tells us everything about the relative values attached to alternative aims, such as having more consumption rather than more spare time, and against what trade-off; the values attached to more consumption rather than more investment, including education. A long list of other possible components of social welfare could be given, but I will add only one more, of paramount importance, and that is the distribution of consumption and quantity and type of work done among the citizens.

It seems natural that the social welfare function depends on the welfare functions of the various citizens, or at least groups of citizens. Category I of our alternative approaches can be subdivided into five group of approaches. The more generally we formulate our assumptions, the less certain, of course, can we be about the concrete propositions we can make about the features of the optimum.

Group *A* assumes only that social welfare depends on the welfare functions (or values) of all the citizens, but it does not specify how. Groups *B* and *C* assume that the type of dependence is what the mathematicians call separable; this means that social welfare consists of separate portions each depending only on one individual's welfare. In order to keep our treatment simple, we will consider only two forms of separability; Group *B* assumes that social welfare is the weighted sum of the individual welfare values; the weights meaning that a unit of welfare of one person counts more to the policy makers than a welfare unit of another person; or less. In Group C of our approaches we assume that social welfare is the unweighted sum of the individual welfare of each citizen. Obviously this implies that under approach B we discriminate between various persons or groups and under C we do not. The distinction between these two groups only makes sense, however, if we assume that we can measure welfare and that, if there were more than one way of measuring it, we make a choice among these ways. This choice implies ethical elements as well as elements of methodology or philosophy of science. Depending on how we measure individual welfare, the question may even be asked whether not elements of discrimination can also slip in here.

We will discuss two more groups, to be called D and E, based on further assumptions that are conceivable. In these groups we assume that, as an ethical element, some form of equality between human beings is introduced. Before defining equality, we must go into some technicalities of an individual welfare calculation. Such a calculation contains three groups of elements. The first, to be called variables, indicate the size of entities which contribute to the individual's feeling of satisfaction and which can be varied, either by himself or by outside forces. Examples are the quantity of consumption, the quantity of effort made or the job chosen by or given to the individual.

The second group of elements, to be called parameters, are the scores describing the individual's capabilities and needs; capabilities can be described by an IQ, or a set of test results; needs can be described by the size of his family and the state of his health. In the short run these are given and they differ from person to person. In the longer run they can be changed, but behind these changes there will still be unchangeable characteristics.

The third category of elements appearing in a person's welfare function are called coefficients; they indicate how strongly each of the other categories are affecting the person's welfare. In other words, they reflect the individual's sensitivity to the values of or changes in variables and parameters.

In a brief, and therefore always less precise, way we can say that the variables depict the individual's situation, the parameters his quality, and the coefficients his human nature.

What interpretation can we give now to the alleged equality of human beings? Since their variables are (their situation is) subject to change all the time, they are irrelevant for any definition of equality. Since parameters (qualities) are different according to observation, the only possibility of connecting them with the concept of equality is to believe that in the very long run parameters may become equal. A case in point is made by L. Soltow [7] who observed that in Norwegian schools, the scores of children or grandchildren of people with different achievement were, one or two generations later, on the average equal. The most realistic assumption is that the coefficients are the same for all human beings and distinct from those of other animals. Our groups of approaches D and E are therefore characterized by the assumptions that, respectively, the parameters and the coefficients are the same for each individual, or for each relevant group of individuals (Group D) and the coefficients only (Group E) are the same for individuals or groups. Relevant groups, in this context, are groups which are treated equally by the institutions characterizing the optimum order.

Category II deals with the various sets of restrictions we can introduce. This category too can be subdivided into various groups of approaches; we will indicate these with the aid of lowercase letters. Some of the restrictions are of a technical nature: They express either production techniques or other natural laws, such as the equality of the quantities available and the quantities given a destination (consumption, investment). An essential difference in approach is found here just by considering production techniques without external effects (Group a) and in also considering techniques with these effects (Group b). A production technique or process will be said to show external effects if its level of activity influences not only the welfare of sellers and buyers of the product, but also the welfare of others ("outsiders"). If no outsiders' welfare is affected, the process does not show external effects.

Other restrictions may be introduced as part of the objectives of the social welfare function. If such objectives are absent, we will speak of Group c; if there are, we speak of Group d. An important example of the latter is the restriction that all individual welfare values are wanted to be equal, which will be our definition of justice, coinciding with the definition chosen by Kolm [4].

4. Some Remarks on the Consequences of Various Approaches

No reader will be astonished if we state, as we did, that the more general our assumptions are, the less we can conclude in the form of propositions about the optimum. We will indicate some of these various conclusions for a set of approaches where, for the time being, we disregard the existence of different goods and consumptive services. In the models we now have in mind, the existence of only one consumer good is supposed, in which we express consumable income. Another simplification is that we are not dealing with the development over time of the various entities we are going to discuss. Although these simplifications look formidable, they are not. It is relatively easy to introduce more goods or more time units. Our focus will be on other aspects of the optimum order, namely, the organizational ones.

We will now discuss very briefly the kind of propositions which can be made under the groups of approaches defined before (IA to IE and IIa to IId). In Group IA, where nothing in particular was assumed about how social welfare depends on the various individual welfare values, and where no external effects are present, we can prove that in the optimum position the ratio of the marginal utility of income to the marginal utility of a given type of effort is equal for all individuals. The marginal utility of effort can be seen as a way to measure marginal costs of production. Therefore our proposition may be interpreted also by stating that competitive markets for commodities and factors are institutions which together can produce the optimum, provided that also the other characteristics of the optimum are fulfilled. The latter proviso refers especially to income distribution which must also be optimal. In Group IA no more precise definition of the optimal income distribution can be given than equality among individuals of the marginal personal utility of income, multiplied by the marginal social utility of a unit increase in personal utility. If a larger number of products and of production factors is considered, Group IA can derive similar propositions for all of them, with the same proviso on income distribution; a proviso comparable with an "empty box," as long as we are not more specific.

For Group IB, where again no externalities are assumed to exist, but social welfare is defined as a weighted sum of individual welfare values, the weights being constant for each individual, the same type of propositions can be attained, but the income distribution needed can be defined slightly more explicitly; equality among individuals is now required of their marginal income utilities multiplied by a fixed weight characteristic for each person.

Again, a more concrete proposition is possible under the assumptions of Group IC; free markets will lead to the optimum, provided that the income distribution is such that all persons have equal marginal utilities of income.

Group IE, where persons are assumed equal in every respect, would require equal incomes for everybody; supposedly at most only a future possibility and not necessarily so; in the short run, Group ID makes the more realistic assumption of equality in coefficients, meaning that incomes should be equal after correction for differences in needs, both professional and purely human needs.

In all that precedes we assumed the absence of external effects, as formulated under Group IIa.

If we introduce the assumptions of Group IIb, free markets will not guarantee the arrival at the optimum for those goods the production of which shows external effects. In some way producers must be induced to take into account these effects; this may be done by taxes or subsidies in some cases, but in other cases central planning and decisions will be needed. In the well-known example provided by Meade, concerning mutual external effects between honey production and apple production, integration of the two activities into one enterprise would solve the problem and leave free markets as a possibility.

The preceding solutions are those valid for Group IIc, where no other restrictions were assumed to exist. In Group IId, where we add to the maximization of social utility the requirement of justice, defined as equality between the personal welfare values, Waardenburg [16] has shown that the same requirements with regard to income distribution are needed as in Group IB, that is, the equality of individual marginal utilities multiplied by a personal weight. Presumably in this case higher weights will be given to individuals whose personal parameters would mean a handicap in a free society.

5. Illustration by a Critical Appraisal of Traditional Welfare Economics and its Practical Application

I am aware of the rather abstract character of what I said so far. I am now going to use everyday language to illustrate my points. This I propose to do by first giving a critical appraisal of the contents of and the practical applications made with the aid of traditional welfare economics.

Among the positive results of traditional welfare economics as well as their use by politicians I want to mention the propositions that in a large number of situations price uniformity for a given product or a given production factor (capital or many types of labor) is a feature of the optimum. When seen as a plea against discrimination in pricing, and against import duties levied by rich countries, such propositions often have been very useful. If we add that these uniform prices must be equal to the marginal costs, another useful case is made against monopolies or oligopolies.

A negative aspect of the way in which these results have been presented and abused by politicians is, however, that the important corollary was overlooked with regard to income distribution. The nondiscrimination and antitrust interpretations often given are valid only if the income distribution also is optimal. This is what I meant when I stressed that the optimum social order is a complete set of institutions the behavior equations of which, taken together, cover all the optimum conditions of welfare economics.

It is worthwhile to repeat this in simpler language still, by saying that, in an overwhelming majority of situations, incomes that are obtained from free activities must be redistributed before being spent. There is no rule for the optimum which says that any rich man is permitted to spend his productive income all for himself or, the other way round, a poor individual only has the right to spend as little as his or her low productive income permits. A system of taxes and subsidies is part of the optimum. By subsidies we may also understand the supply of services at lower prices than their costs. This is true within each nation, among the richer and the poorer strata; it is equally true between nations—even more so, since primary (or productive) income inequality is much larger between than within nations. Here reality is terribly far from the optimum.

The supply of services at prices below costs as well as what has been called central planning and decision making, together with other activities may be subsumed under the heading "tasks of public authorities." Contrary to what ultra-liberalists and similar doctrinaire politicians have said, there has been an impressive shift of tasks from private to public decision makers. Some public tasks are taken for granted nowadays by everyone, although there have been times when even these were carried out by private bodies or persons, for instance the tasks of army and police. Education, once a private activity, is increasingly being financed by public authorities. Road maintenance, except for turnpikes, has become a public responsibility. Railways in most countries are now publicly owned. Agricultural and other unstable markets are regulated. The total level of demand is determined by anticyclical and development policies of public authorities. New tasks have been added in the field of health; quite recently antipollution measures have been taken, with, in some respects, the United States leading. In the field of information, such as broadcasting and television, statistical and other public authorities make important contributions.

I cannot resist the temptation here to insert a remark on what have been called public goods. Thinking of processes which satisfy needs by their production of goods, my preference is to hold that not the character of the goods, but rather that of the process determines whether these needs are satisfied by private or by public activities. There is a tendency for public authorities, or at least publicly owned or controlled units to carry out processes with very high fixed costs, whereas processes with lower fixed costs can be be left to the decisions of private people. Cars tend to be private, trains and planes public; theatres private, television public, and so on.

Once we agree that income redistribution is an element of the optimal social order and taxes play an important part in redistribution, we must face the fact that the overwhelming part of our taxes are of a nonoptimal type: they affect marginal gains to be obtained from additional production considered and imply a downward bias of production.

6. Outline of Interdisciplinary Approach

Let me now try to elaborate on the positive aspects of an alternative method to arrive at some propositions concerning the optimal social order. Methodologically I prefer to approach the structure of the "best" order by a number of successive steps, from simpler to more complicated models

—a method not unknown to economic science and often applied by other sciences as well. I want to stress that such a successive approximation has not only a didactic value, but, in my opinion, should be part and parcel of a scientific approach with a view to make matters not more complicated than is needed to remain in touch with reality, that is, observation. If a simpler theory can explain, in sufficient detail, observed phenomena relevant to our problem, there is no need to use a more complicated theory. I know how popular the joke about some of my colleagues is who reported to think "Why make something simple if you can also make it complicated?" I am not only opposing them for didactic reasons, but in principle.

The first stage of our task consists, as already pointed out, of the choice of a social welfare function. My proposal is to take the sum of individual welfare values, without weights attached. To me this seems to reflect democracy without discrimination, without assuming that people are attaching a high value to sacrificing much to others, but assuming that our attitude toward others should be governed also slightly only by envy. In other words, feelings of solidarity just about cancel feelings of envy.

Methodologically my proposal presupposes, of course, a tremendous optimism with regard to the possibility of measuring various people's welfare. Let me defend my position as follows. Of course, I know that we do not have a good thermometer for welfare today. We only have a very defective one in that we can agree only in extreme cases that one individual's welfare is lower than another's. Today we only have a restricted number of wise women or men who are able to pass more precise judgments (and this is what measuring means) on the relative welfare of different people. In order to reduce the errors in such judgments, we take the average of the judgments of a fairly large number of observers, hoping that the errors will be mutually independent and partly cancel each other. We decide in parliament or in other groups by majority vote; for very important decisions we require qualified majorities—up to 85 percent in IMF—when we vote on creating Special Drawing Rights. All this is not exactly what we understand by objective or scientific measurement. As already suggested, we then think of thermometers, for instance. We should be aware, however, of the fact that also the measurement of temperature in physics is not a unanimous decision. Between 4° centigrade and 0° most substances agree that there is a fall of 4° in temperature, but if we had taken a water column as a thermometer in that case, water would tell us the temperature had gone up. In other words, even in physics we have taken a majority vote without insisting on unanimity. My optimism on the future measurement of welfare is based on a general belief in scientific progress and on the state of affairs with regard to some components of welfare, such as health, where medical experts feel already fairly confident in comparing different individuals.

When it comes to specifying in explicit mathematical shape my concept of welfare I am inclined to use Weber-Fechner's law and propose that the welfare feeling derived from income available per consumer rises with the logarithm of that income [12], that is, by equal steps for equal percentage increases of income. In addition, I tend to state that an individual's happiness (as far as relevant for socioeconomic policies) depends on the possible tension (difference) between his actual capability and the capability required by his job. Usually he will take a job not too far from what his capabilities correspond with, and the tensions will not be large. But his happiness will decline rapidly if the tension increases in absolute value. As in job evaluation, we may use, to characterize the job as well as the person, more than one, up to twenty different aspects. Recently, some have reduced the number because of fairly high intercorrelations between several of the aspects used. Brinkmann [1], for the description of more qualified jobs, still uses a large number of aspects, but my guess is that there also we can reduce the number. Since the job aspects and the corresponding personal abilities are the parameters in the welfare function, we still do not have the coefficients. Here I see a program of measurements in order to test my assumption that the coefficients are roughly the same for everybody, which then would reflect the "fundamental equality of men." We have begun to make the measurements, but they are in a very preliminary stage only. They probably will inform us about changes we will have to make and new parameters we must add.

Be this as it is, the remainder of my discussion will be based on the assumption that welfare or utility values can be measured and hence added and that we can establish a social welfare function. We may want to add, at least as one alternative, the restriction of justice, as discussed before. We must add, anyway, a considerable number of technical, chemical, and other restrictions; today we can add many more even than we thought twenty years ago. The extension given by Leontief [5] to his earlier work on input-output analysis is illustrative of some of the additional restrictions we have to take into account.

For activities showing no external effects we will find that a free market can still be a useful institution to allocate production factors and consumption, provided that other institutions are created or operating simultaneously. Decisions on activities with important external effects cannot be left to decisions of independent firms or consumers. They must be induced to take decisions in the general interest which in these cases does not coincide with the traditional private interest. We already saw that sometimes taxes or subsidies may be sufficient; but there are other cases where more centralized decisions are needed, from the simple integration of two activities (honey and apple production) to the full-fledged decisions at the national level and even the world level—the latter type being much more rare than our survival requires [8].

Moreover an important income redistribution is required. As I tried to show elsewhere [9] this redistribution can hardly be stopped at the point of taxation, where we are now. Taxes on capabilities or capacities, so-called lump-sum taxes, are the only ones in line with the optimum conditions. Income taxes are a second-best at most. In the real optimum order, persons should be taxed on the scores obtained in an ability test which may be used also for providing them with the jobs they are most appropriate for. Such tests are not yet available in a sufficiently accurate form. But we observe continual progress in testing persons and designing their career. In order to take account of an individual's performance as well of errors made in earlier tests, his testing may have to be repeated every five or ten years. The essence of the lump-sum tax based on a person's capability test is that the full fruits of any additional effort he makes will be left to him. Under such a regime two incentives will work simultaneously to let a capable man work hard. If he does not work hard, the high tax he has to pay will leave him with a low income; if he works hard, the full fruits of that hard work will be his.

Most people, including myself, are sceptical about the benefits to be derived from introducing such a new tax in the near future. We do not have the reliable tests that would be required if we are to give them such a central place. For the time being, taxes on wealth and hence inheritance taxes are components of a lump-sum tax which can be used. But they hit the wealthy only and not the gifted. In future, if our tests can be improved, a modest experiment with them could be made, where simultaneously such a tax at a moderate scale could be started and the rates of income tax lowered so as to yield the same revenue to the treasury. With increasing experience we hopefully could continue that substitution.

The case made for a capability tax constitutes an example where, at present, the costs (in money and in trouble) are too high for the institution to be introduced. It is comparable with the position of most developing (and some developed) countries vis-à-vis income taxes. The people of these countries do not yet have the tax collectors and the tax morals needed for income taxes to be levied reasonably well, and hence they must concentrate on indirect taxes, farther apart still from the optimum.

With the lump-sum tax just described, based on a capability test, we can equalize the level of living for the various groups of society to a greater extent than is the case now. Elsewhere I elaborated on the features of an optimal income redistribution [12], and I already have repeated here that income differences would mainly reflect differences in needs, professional and personal. Professional needs may involve financing a study or repaying a fellowship. Personal needs include the size of the family and the health of the individual considered.

7. Concluding Remarks

I tried to unfold my views on how to shape an optimal social order. I emphasized the interdisciplinary approach needed to define and specify such an order. I did not consider social welfare functions imposed by a country's government; but I want to add that certain features may have to be imposed if the population is shortsighted. Myopia is common to all of us in some sense, and may cause an individual to make decisions he might deplore later on. Forestalling such decisions is a legitimate area for government to impose some measures. The best-known examples are obligatory schooling up to a certain age or excises on consumer goods endangering health, such as tobacco, alcoholic drinks, and a number of drugs. Imposing the complete pattern of production, as was done in Eastern Europe until 1956, or during wartime everywhere, leaves such a gap between the preferences of the government and those of the population that I excluded it from my treatment of the optimum order. If the pessimists of the Club of Rome are right, we may, however, have to consider the kind of order such imposition implies. In a way, I have been slightly more optimistic, by introducing the concerns of the Club of Rome in a number of new restrictions we have to reckon with.

Even so I have come to conclusions about the best order which have several socialist features: increasing tasks for public authorities, a much less unequal distribution of disposable income by higher taxes on wealth and the recognition of needs as one base for income differences. Interestingly enough I have arrived at these conclusions even though the concept of the social welfare function used was not formulated beforehand with a preference for any particular type of income distribution. If justice, defined as equal welfare for all, is added, an income distribution may well result which implies higher incomes for heavy physical or extremely dull work than for mental or interesting work; but this case has not been analyzed in my lecture.

If it can be assumed that the lump-sum tax based on capability will once become possible, our optimal order may become more egalitarian and at the same time more efficient than it is in presentday Eastern European societies. This illustrates that the stubborn adherence to socialization of all means of production is more a demonstration of faithfulness to a century-old doctrine than one of original thinking. Of course this can only be substantiated if we actually succeed in testing a person's capability more precisely. With all the work done and progress made in both job evaluation and career planning—interestingly enough first in business—I am not without hope that we will succeed in introducing capability as a tax base.

There are other ways open for us to equalize income distribution to a greater extent, however. As I tried to show in a few recent publications [13, 15], schooling and family planning can have an impact on income distribution, and it is conceivable that inequality of incomes can be further reduced.

I want to finish by returning to my introductory remarks on the aim of my research. As I see it, modernized research of an interdisciplinary character, using the framework of welfare economics, can be used as a common scientific language for social scientists all over the globe. It is my contention that Eastern European and Chinese social scientists could clarify their own position if they take the pains of a scientific critique of the approach offered; so far only ideologists have done so. Elsewhere I have attempted to answer these critics [14]. If we really want to coexist, a better mutual understanding is needed. It has to begin with scientists.

Notes

1. L. Brinkmann, *Der Einfluss der Ausbildung auf des Gehalt von aussertariflch bezahlten Angestelten der Wirtschaft*, Mitteilungen aus der Arbeitsmarkt—und Berufsforschung, 3 (1970), pp. 124 ff.

2. J. W. Forrester, *World Dynamics*, Cambridge, Mass., 1971.

3. H. Kahn and A. J. Wiener, *The Year 2000*, New York, 1967.

4. S.-G. Kolm, *Justice et équité*, CEPREMAP, Paris (mimeographed).

5. W. Leontief and D. Ford, *Air Pollution and the Economic Structure: Empirical Results of Input-Output Computations*, Fifth Conference on Input-Output Techniques, Geneva, 1971 (mimeographed).

6. L. Meadows, "The Predicament of Mankind," *The Futurist*, V (1971), p. 137.

7. L. Soltow, *Towards Income Equality in Norway,* Madison, Milwaukee, Wisc., 1965.

8. Survival, Conference on Human, Charles F. Kettering Foundation, Dayton, Ohio, 1970.

9. J. Tinbergen, "Should the Income Tax be among the Means of Economic Policy?" in *Til Frederik Zeuthen,* Copenhagen, 1958, p. 351 ff.

10. ———, *Selected Papers,* Amsterdam, 1959, pp. 264 ff.

11. ———, "The Significance of Welfare Economics for Socialism," in *Essays in Honour of Oskar Lange,* Warsaw, 1964, pp. 591 ff.

12. ———, "A Positive and a Normative Theory of Income Distribution," *The Review of Income and Wealth,* 16 (1970), p. 221.

13. ———, "Trends in Income Distribution in Some Western Countries," to be published in Geneva International Essays, Geneva, 1972.

14. ———, "The Impact of Education on Income Distribution," to be published.

15. ———, "Once Again Welfare Economics," *Coexistence,* 9 (1972).

16. J. G. Waardenburg, diss. (to be published).

PRODUCTIVITY UNDER TWO SYSTEMS: THE USSR VERSUS THE WEST *

Abram Bergson

Introduction

Economics today abounds in weighty issues, but few can be more so than the proverbial one concerning the comparative economic merit of rival social systems. Of particular interest, however, are the two great systems that now so nearly dominate the world. The relative economic merit of entire social systems such as socialism and capitalism is a large and complex issue. We must be optimistic to think that we shall ever be able to settle it at all definitively.

We have, however, gained some insight into the question from scholarly studies made through the years. At least, if we are at all detached, we know better than we did before how to evaluate the more extravagant of partisan pronouncements on it. Needless to say there has been no lack of such pronouncements on either side. Perhaps further investigation can narrow the range of speculation still more.

I report summarily on the results of some research to that end. Economic merit has many facets. My concern will be with but one of them, but a by no means unimportant one.

In technical economic writings, productive efficiency is construed variously. I focus on that standard on the understanding that reference is being made to the degree to which a country produces the volume of output of which it is theoretically capable. What a country is theoretically capable of in that respect depends on the quantity and quality of the productive factors and the knowledge of technologies for combining them that are available to it. Productive efficiency is a somewhat intricate concept, but it may suffice here to underline what is in any event rather familiar: A country may indeed fail to realize its theoretic productive capacity because of the nature of its economic working arrangements; because, that is, of defective managerial and labor incentives, and because of deficiencies of one kind or another in coordination of enterprises and industries, whether the coordination is achieved through markets or planning, or both. Productive efficiency is properly viewed, therefore, as a standard for appraising economic working arrangements. I shall so view it here.

How may we gauge productive efficiency? Usually, when the concern has been to do so, an attempt has been made to delineate patterns of behavior induced by the economic working arrangements, and somehow to contrast such patterns with corresponding theoretic norms of productive efficiency. Divergencies observed between the behavior patterns and theoretic norms then signify inefficiency. Such inquiries have long been a familiar feature in the study of capitalism, and by now have often been undertaken in the study of socialism as well. The results have been illuminating, and it is in part through such studies that we have gained the insight we now have into the comparative economic merit of the two systems.

I propose, however, to explore another and relatively novel approach to comparative productive efficiency. In order to gauge that aspect, I shall refer primarily to comparative data on levels of productivity in different countries. Productivity and productive efficiency, while sometimes taken to be one and the same, are not really such. A country's productivity may well be relatively high or low because its economic working arrangements are efficient or inefficient. But, its productivity may be relatively high or low for other reasons as well. As we need not ponder long to see that is so even where, as here, reference is to data on productivity more or less comprehensive of the economy generally, and also to measures not only of a usual type, on output per worker, but of the kind that only lately have come into use, that is measures of output per composite unit of labor and capital together, or "factor productivity." But, granting that all such measures may diverge from productive efficiency, they can, I think, still shed light on that matter.

Socialism and capitalism are understood here, as they usually are, primarily in terms of the locus of preponderant ownership of the means of production. Under either system, however, institutions, policies, and practices for the conduct of economic affairs may still vary. Moreover, depending on such economic working arrangements, economic performance, including productive efficiency, may vary as well.

We must understand accordingly, the particular comparisons of productivity that are to be made. For that purpose, I consider only one among all the socialist countries in the world today. The USSR, nevertheless, is certainly a particularly interesting socialist country. It is clearly preeminent among socialist countries generally. Furthermore, its famous system of centralist planning and its economic policies have been widely copied elsewhere, not only in broad outline but in detail.

Among capitalist countries, I shall refer to the United States, France, Germany (the Federal Republic, of course), the United Kingdom, and Italy. The economies of these countries, as with those of the capitalist world generally, are all decidedly mixed, and quite remote from the pure laissez-faire, private enterprise systems of textbooks. Economic working arrangements, nevertheless, often vary in detail from one of these countries to another. These circumstances must be borne in mind.

The data compiled on productivity relate to 1960. For present purposes, this seems to have been a fairly usual year in the USSR. Farm output there, however, was several percent below the peak level of 1958. Among the Western countries considered, 1960 was marked everywhere by an expansion of output to new high levels. Some countries, however, especially the United States and Italy, were experiencing significant unemployment. These facts, too, will have to be considered.

While the approach adopted is relatively new, I myself have already made several studies such as the one now being undertaken.[1] A further inquiry, however, has resulted in additional and more or less novel calculations and will also permit me to take account of some further thoughts.

To compare productivity in different countries is a formidable task, but one need not aspire to an impossible statistical certitude to feel it worth undertaking. I explain sources and methods in an Appendix, but I should note here that I have benefited especially from the well-known, recent work of Edward F. Denison on Western economic growth.[2] In the compilation of the comparative data to be considered, his calculations again and again served as an invaluable point of departure.

Productivity in the Economy Generally

As implied, the comparative data that I have compiled on productivity levels are inexact, but productivity in the different countries studied should vary broadly as found (Table 1). Thus, among the Western countries considered, the United States clearly surpasses all others. Next, and more or less on a par with each other, though far below the United States, are our three Northwest European countries: France, Germany, and the United Kingdom. And much below even these countries is our remaining Western country, Italy.

These comparative relations are observed whether reference is to output per worker or to output per composite unit of labor and capital, that is, factor productivity. The latter yardstick,

TABLE 1
GROSS MATERIAL PRODUCT PER EMPLOYED WORKER AND PER UNIT OF FACTOR INPUTS, SELECTED COUNTRIES, 1960[a]
(USA = 100 percent)

	Gross Material product per Employed Worker (1)	Gross material product per unit of factor (labor and reproducible capital) input (2)
United States	100	100
France	51	63
Germany	51	65
United Kingdom	49	64
Italy	34	47
USSR	31	41

a) Gross material product represents gross domestic product exclusive of output originating in selected final services: health care, education, government administration, defense, and housing. In the comparison between the USSR and the USA, however, reference is to gross national rather than gross domestic product.

Employment is, throughout, exclusive of workers employed in the services referred to, except for housing. In the calculation of factor productivity, reproducible capital employed in all such services, including housing, is omitted.

Output and, in the calculation of factor productivity, factor inputs are valued at US dollar prices. In the comparison of Western European countries and the United States, valuation of output is at factor cost, and in that of the USSR and the United States, at market price. Employment is adjusted for hours, additional hours beyond those worked by a US nonfarm worker in 1960 being counted less than proportionately. For sources and methods, see the Appendix.

however, is decidedly the more favorable one for all the Western European countries when they are compared with the United States.

I have referred to Western countries. As for the USSR, that ranks with Italy at the bottom of our list. That too is so whichever the yardstick. The USSR, however, is essentially on a par with Italy in respect of output per worker, but appears to fall perceptibly below that country in respect of factor productivity.

In all these comparisons, a country's output is essentially its national income or output before the deduction of depreciation, but exclusive of output originating in diverse services, particularly education, health care, government administration, defense, and housing. Correspondingly, in relating output to employment of labor, on the one hand, and to such employment and the available capital stock, on the other, I refer to the amounts of both factors used in the economy generally, exclusive of those service sectors.

Our comparative data, then, relate to productivity in the economy generally, apart from the indicated service sectors. International comparisons of productivity are often made that include services such as are in question, but in convential national income accounting output in such sectors is actually measured only by factor inputs. For this reason, as practitioners have long been aware, inclusion of such sectors tends only to obscure, rather than illuminate, differences in economic performance. They are, therefore, properly omitted here. I refer to services apart from housing, but for one reason or another, that sector seems to be rather special everywhere. Comparative productivity in it, therefore, is best left to separate inquiry.

In view of the indicated omissions, my comparative data are appropriately referred to as relating to gross material product per worker and per composite unit of labor and capital. Those familiar with the famous Soviet concept of national income will be aware that I have in effect delineated national income here in a manner more or less comparable to that which is customary in the USSR. The Soviet concept of national income has often been criticized in the West, often with good reason, but for purposes of productivity calculations such as are in question it has its point.[3]

In my calculations, output and, where in order, factor inputs are, of course, in comparable prices. Specifically, valuation throughout is in terms of US dollar prices.[4]

Output per worker is the most usual representation of productivity. But the alternative and more novel one of output per composite unit of labor and capital is decidedly the more interesting one here. Output per worker may vary between countries simply because workers in one country are equipped with relatively more capital than they are in another, and without productive efficiency of economic working arrangements being any greater in one case than in the other. By comparing instead output per composite unit of labor and capital, we in effect allow for such differences in capital stock per worker. Our data should be seen in that light.

Sources of Productivity Differences

For our purposes, however, factor productivity too has its limitations. To begin with, labor may differ in quality in different countries. So far as it does factor productivity too will vary without productive efficiency necessarily being any greater in one country than in another. Were it not for the difference in labor quality, the economic working arrangements of one country might really function quite as well as even very different economic working arrangements in another. Two outstanding causes of differences in labor quality, however, are differences in education and sex. If we allow for such differences in a way made familiar by Denison and indeed by use of adjustment coefficients he himself has applied in such calculations, we see that all Western countries other than the United States again gain on that country (Table 2). They compare with each other, however, much as before. That is so whether the yardstick is labor or factor productivity. The Soviet Union also gains on the United States at this point. It is still more or less on a par with Italy in labor productivity, however, and somewhat below that country in factor productivity.

Denison's adjustment coefficients supposedly

TABLE 2
GROSS MATERIAL PRODUCT PER EMPLOYED WORKER AND PER UNIT OF FACTOR INPUTS, WITH EMPLOYMENT ADJUSTED FOR QUALITY, SELECTED COUNTRIES, 1960[a]
(USA = 100 percent)

	Gross material product per employed worker (1)	Gross material product per unit of factor (labor and reproducible capital) inputs (2)
United States	100	100
France	60	70
Germany	61	75
United Kingdom	54	68
Italy	44	57
USSR	42	51

a) Employment adjusted throughout for differences in education, and sex and age structure, as well as hours. See the text. For sources and methods, see the Appendix.

represent the comparative earning capacity of workers at different educational levels and of different sexes. I refer to earning capacity in terms of the US experience. Such coefficients are appropriately applied here not only to the United States but to other countries, for to repeat, my calculations generally are in US dollar prices. As Denison would be the first to admit, however, the coefficients are crude, and my results must be so also. Particularly dubious, I suspect, is the allowance for differences in sex structure. This entails discounting female relatively to male workers by 41 percent. That conforms to the average difference in earning between female and male workers in the United States, but even a male chauvinist must concede that the differential probably often reflects limitations in employment opportunities open to women rather than the inherent qualitative inferiority of their labor. To the extent that it does, my calculations tend to be unduly favorable to the USSR. In the Soviet Union, women are employed to a far greater degree than in any other country considered. They now constitute one-half of the Soviet labor force. In the West the corresponding figure is one-fourth to one-third. An inordinately high discount for female labor would overstate calculated productivity for the USSR relative to that for other countries.

Factor productivity may also vary because

workers do not work as hard in one country as in another. To what extent is that so here? According to the authority on productivity to whom I have already referred: [5]

It seems to me probable that differences in effort are partially responsible for a higher level of output in the United States than in Europe. . . . But the quantitative importance of differences in intensity of work I find impossible to judge, much less to measure by any direct approach.

Reference is only to Western countries, but the degree to which effort might differ between the USSR and the West is, needless to say, also obscure. According to a familiar socialist claim, under public ownership of the means of production, the worker might be expected to exert himself with notable diligence. The Soviet worker no doubt has sometimes done so, but among workers, as among the population generally, ideological zeal seems for long to have been on the wane. Perhaps effort is, if anything, usually greater in the USA than in the USSR, though that is conjectural.

In whatever way effort differs among countries, productivity should differ correspondingly.

Effort, however, may differ because of differences in incentive arrangements, the arrangements in one country being more beneficent than those in another. If so, the difference in effort might properly be construed as manifesting a difference in productive efficiency as well, so there would be no incongruity after all between such efficiency and productivity. However, effort may vary simply because of differences in worker preferences for labor and leisure, and without incentive arrangements being any more or less beneficent in one country than another. In that case, productive efficiency would be the same despite the observed difference in productivity. It would be understood that the economic working arrangements prevailing in different countries simply satisfied different preferences between work and earnings. They might do that just as they might satisfy different preferences among consumers' goods. If differences in effort are difficult to gauge, however, comparative causes of such differences are no less so. Our comparative data on productivity must be viewed accordingly.[6]

In calculating factor productivity, I have referred in the case of labor inputs only to workers actually employed. Such a calculation has its point, but in judging comparative productive efficiency we must consider the fact already noted: At the time studied, among Western countries, the USA and Italy were experiencing significant amounts of unemployment. Relative to the gaps in productivity that have been observed, however, the differences in unemployment rates were nevertheless very limited (Table 3). As for the

TABLE 3
UNEMPLOYMENT RATES, ADJUSTED TO US DEFINITIONS, SELECTED COUNTRIES, 1960[a]

	Unemployment Labor Force (percent)
United States	5.6
France	1.9
Germany	1.0
United Kingdom	2.4
Italy	4.3

a) President's Committee to Appraise Employment and Unemployment Statistics, *Measuring Employment and Unemployment* (Washington, D.C. 1962), p. 220.

USSR, it is often claimed that in that country unemployment has been abolished. In fact, unemployment of the cyclical sort familiar in the West is no doubt little known. In the USSR as in the West, however, there is, of course, structural and frictional unemployment, though how much is difficult to judge.[7]

For capital, inputs have been measured by the entire stock, whether utilized or not. Capital may be utilized with varying intensity, however, and at least beyond a point, more intensive use is

by no means costless. Hence, should productivity
be high merely because of more intensive use,
that need not betoken anything like a correspondingly high productive efficiency. It should be observed, therefore, that productivity in the USSR
is low despite the fact that capital there is used
notably intensively. At least that is so in industry.
In the USSR at the time studied, 35 percent of
industrial workers were employed in other than
the first shift. In the USA the corresponding figure was 23 percent; in Northwest Europe about
10 percent, and in Italy 16 percent.[8]

In the case of capital, I have referred only
to that of a reproducible sort. Hence, productive
efficiency apart, productivity may also vary because of differences in the quality and location
of natural resources. Needless to say, there are
such differences not only among the Western
countries studied but as between the USSR and
such countries. There are nevertheless reasons to
think that they could not in any case account for
any large part of the observed differences in productivity, but this is an intricate matter on which
we still have much to learn.[9]

Productivity may also differ, without any corresponding variation in productive efficiency, due
to differential opportunities to exploit economies of scale. Such opportunities turn on market
size, which is not, of course, the same thing as size
of the country, for transportation costs and access

to foreign markets also matter. Moreover, in industry economies of scale are associated to a great extent with the size of production units. Where they are, they probably can be largely realized with plants of only relatively modest size.[10] Such economies, nevertheless, are not always realized, but a failure to realize them, while lowering productivity, is properly seen as reducing productive efficiency as well.[11] In any event, the USSR should not be at any disadvantage at this point. Compared to the Western European countries studied, it may well be favored.

In sum, productive efficiency is indeed not the same thing as productivity, and it is not easy to gauge one thing from the other. The presumption is, though, that productive efficiency varies widely even among Western countries. But the Soviet performance still does not seem especially distinguished in that light. Most likely, it is matched, if not surpassed, in the West even where productive efficiency is at its lowest.

Productivity and the Stage of Development

But, granting that, are we not concerned with the comparative productive efficiency not merely of the USSR and the Western countries studied, but of socialism and capitalism, or at least of the variants of those social systems found in those countries? From that standpoint, must we not consider that even similar economic working arrangements may perform differently depending on historical and cultural factors? Indeed, is that not already indicated by the differences in factor productivity observed among Western countries? What in particular of the possibility that such differences essentially reflect differences in the stage of economic development in those countries? If so, may not the relatively low factor productivity in the USSR also be due simply to the less-advanced stage of development of that country? So far as productive efficiency is low in the USSR, therefore, may not the cause be the less-advanced stage of development rather than any intrinsic inferiority in socialist centralist planning, as found there?

The questions are in order. Regrettably we have only five observations on factor productivity under capitalism and only one on factor productivity under socialism. These hardly suffice for us to make any very firm generalizations on the relation of factor productivity and the stage of economic development. But among the Western countries studied factor productivity does vary positively with one of two plausible indicators of the stage of development, capital stock per worker (Table 4; Charts 1 and 2).[12] Very possibly it also

TABLE 4
INDICATORS OF THE STAGE OF ECONOMIC DEVELOPMENT AND FACTOR PRODUCTIVITY, SELECTED COUNTRIES, 1960 [a]

	Share of non-agricultural branches in total employment (percent) (1)	Capital stock per worker with labor		Factor productivity, with labor	
		Unadjusted for quality (USA = 100) (2)	Adjusted for quality (USA = 100) (3)	Unadjusted for quality (USA = 100) (4)	Adjusted for quality (USA = 100) (5)
United States	92.0	100	100	100	100
France	78.6	45	52	63	70
Germany	86.2	36	43	65	75
United Kingdom	95.8	35	39	64	68
Italy	68.0	25	33	47	57
USSR	61.5	34	45	41	51

a) For capital stock per worker, reference is made to reproducible fixed capital and employment in the economy generally, exclusive of selected final services as already described. Employment is adjusted for differences in hours in both variants given. For data on factor productivity, see Tables 1 and 2. For other data, see the Appendix Tables A-1 and A-3.

CHART 1.
Share of Nonfarm Branches in Employment
and Factor Productivity, Selected Countries, 1960

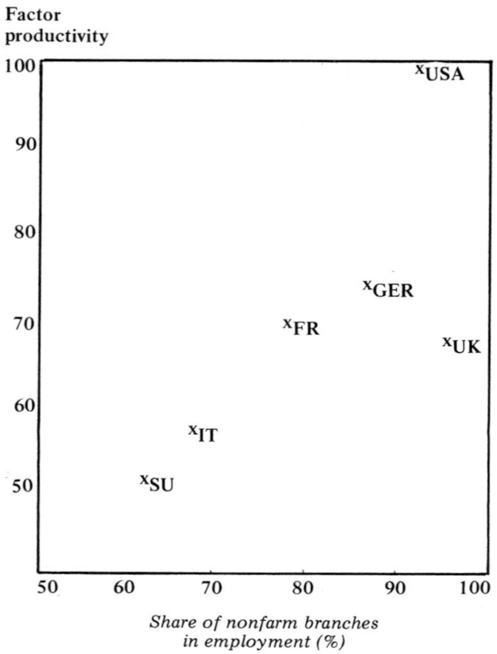

CHART 2.
Capital Stock per Worker and Factor
Productivity, Selected Countries, 1960

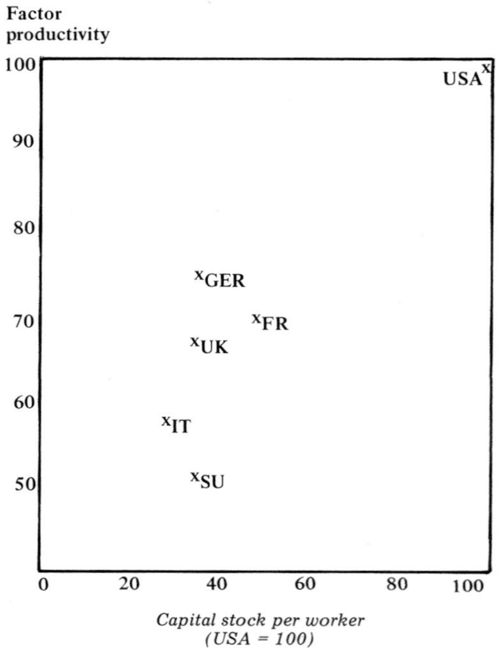

does so with the other, the share of nonfarm branches in total employment. There are, however, marked incongruities in the latter case. Thus, in terms of the share of nonfarm employment, Britain is at a very advanced stage, in fact at an even more advanced stage than the USA. In factor productivity, however, Britain ranks below the USA, and is only more or less on a par with Germany and France. With labor adjusted for quality, it even appears perceptibly below Germany. However, in terms of the same yardstick of development, factor productivity in the United States seems incongruously high.

What of the USSR? So far as there is a systematic relation in Western countries of factor productivity to the development stage when the share of nonfarm employment is the yardstick, the USSR apparently fits well into that pattern. With capital stock per worker as the yardstick, however, the USSR seems not to conform to the Western pattern. The capital stock per worker of the Soviet Union is practically comparable to that of two of our three Northwest European countries, Germany and the United Kingdom, and distinctly above that of Italy. Yet as already seen, factor productivity in the USSR is well below that in all of our Northwest European countries. Soviet factor productivity appears to fall to some extent below even that of Italy.

Of our two yardsticks of the stage of economic development, that represented by the share of nonfarm branches in total employment is the more familiar. For our purposes, however, it is subject to an important deficiency: The yardstick itself is apt to be affected by productive efficiency, particularly in respect of the choice of investment projects in industry. I shall have more to say in a moment about this matter, well known to students of economic development. The alternative yardstick of capital stock per worker is free from any such deficiency, but it too has its limitations, for the data compiled on it are especially inexact.[13]

To come, then, to the larger issue of interest, factor productivity in the USSR may well be relatively low to some extent because of the still not very advanced stage of economic development in that country, rather than because of any intrinsic deficiencies in socialist centralist planning. It is not clear, though, that the low Soviet factor productivity is fully explicable in such terms. The comparative productive efficiency of socialist centralist planning as found in the USSR must be seen accordingly. The performance is clearly better than it appeared initially, though it still cannot be considered especially distinguished by Western standards.

Even these tentative observations put a heavy burden on the limited and imprecise data at hand.[14] It may be useful, even so, to pursue somewhat further the intriguing question posed concerning the relation of factor productivity and the stage of economic development. Are there indeed reasons to think that one aspect should be related to the other?

There no doubt are, but the relation might also be expected often to differ, as our data suggest it does, under such disparate economic working arrangements as are being considered. Thus, a cardinal reason why factor productivity might vary with the development stage turns on the relation of population to resources in agriculture. For historical reasons that relation may be unfavorable, so that an inordinately large labor force works in agriculture at an inordinately low productivity. By the same token, productivity in the economy generally is also depressed. And that may be so whatever the economic working arrangements, but how great the "excess" labor in agriculture is at any time must depend on how rapidly it had been absorbed into industry previously as development proceeded. That must depend among other things on the choice of technologies for new investment projects there. Should these have been unduly "capital intensive," for example, the rate of absorption of farm labor into industry would necessarily have been slowed. For well-known reasons, revolving partly about the improper accounting for capital under an obsolete labor theory of value, industrial investment projects probably have been unduly capital intensive in the USSR.[15] One wonders whether the observed incongruity there between our two yardsticks of development, that is, the low share of nonfarm employment relative to the capital stock per worker, may not be due essentially to that fact.

As a country becomes more advanced economically its economy also tends by almost any reckoning to become more complex. Interconnections multiply among an ever increasing number of production units. The number and variety of products also tends to grow disproportionately. Very possibly here too factor productivity is affected, though differentially under different economic working arrangements. At least, what the effect might be, if there should be any to speak of, under a Western market system is not very clear. Under centralist planning, such as prevails under Soviet socialism, however, it is commonly assumed, and I think with good reason, that the effect is apt to be adverse. As the economy becomes more complex, the burden of decision-making on higher planning agencies becomes evermore onerous. That can hardly be favorable to productivity.

As we saw, productive capacity depends on available technological knowledge. That must be true also of factor productivity. Technological knowledge may originate in any country, but it usually does so more often in more advanced than in less advanced countries. New technological discoveries, however, are not easily monopolized. At least among countries that are at all modern, new knowledge discovered in one seems to become available very soon to others. But, to the extent that there is any lag, that might be a further reason for productivity to be lower in less advanced countries. Here too, however, the effect might depend on the economic working arrangements, but whether that has been so and in what ways among the countries studied is admittedly not very clear. In view of well-known facts about the efforts of the USSR to acquire new foreign technologies, there is little reason to think that that country might be especially tardy in that respect. If it is, though, no doubt the reason is to be found at least partly in the well-known Western restrictions on economic relations with the USSR, rather than in any deficiencies in centralist planning there.[16]

The Western countries studied are all capitalist, and economic working arrangements everywhere are broadly similar. But they are not at all the same. Divergencies in such arrangements must also be a source of differences in factor productivity and sometimes, though hardly always, such differences too should be associated with the stage of development. Thus, among the causes of the relatively high US productivity, it is often suggested, are our superior managerial practices

and relatively competitive markets. Of these two
factors, it would be surprising if the first were not
associated in one way or another with stage of
development. The second, though, is not very
easy to construe similarly. Among more advanced
countries, it has often been held that competition
tends to decline as development proceeds.

Where economic working arrangements vary
more or less independently of the development
stage, however, they may still help explain incongruities in the relation of productivity to that aspect. Thus factor productivity in Britain is perhaps not as high as might have been expected for
a country at its stage of development. If that is
so, we may wonder whether the much discussed
restrictive trade union practices of that country
may not be among the more important causes.[17]

Among socialist countries, economic working arrangements also vary, but where the countries are relatively modern, the divergencies seem
only rarely both consequential and clearly related to the stage of development. Perhaps such
a relation would be more pronounced were it not
for the constraints on institutional innovation imposed everywhere by Soviet hegemony, but that
is conjectural, and how factor productivity might
be affected at this point is especially so.[18]

The forces affecting factor productivity that
have been described should all affect productive
efficiency as well. If factor productivity varies

with the stage of development, therefore, so too must productive efficiency, though here too the variation should be different under Western capitalism and socialist centralist planning. Productive efficiency in the Soviet Union must be seen accordingly. I have focused on contemporaneous differences in factor productivity in different countries. Factor productivity no doubt has also varied historically with the stage of development in any one country, but that is another matter, and it is the contemporaneous variation among different countries that is now of particular concern.

Quality of labor is again an issue here. So far as the calculation of labor inputs does not allow sufficiently for differences in quality, factor productivity is necessarily affected. The effect could easily be to cause it to vary with the stage of development. For example, workers learn not only from formal schooling but also by doing. Learning by doing, however, seems beyond the reach of the measurement of labor skill. So far as it is, there is a further reason for factor productivity to be higher in more advanced countries. In this case, however, productive efficiency could not be considered as varying correspondingly. Measured performance would vary because of a qualitative difference in supplies of factors, particularly labor, rather than because of any difference in effectiveness in their use.[19]

While reference has been to the relation of factor productivity to the development stage, our larger concern has been with the explanation of the apparently low Soviet productive efficiency, particularly the degree to which that is characteristic of the socialist system of centralist planning that prevails there. From the same standpoint, must we not consider also that deficiencies in socialist centralist planning in the USSR might be culturally determined, and in complex ways not necessarily related even to the stage of development? If socialist centralist planning does not function too well in the USSR, what, in other words, of the possibility that that system is simply not particularly appropriate for "moody" Russians, but may still be so for other peoples, say "disciplined" Germans? That is sometimes suggested and, despite the clichés, perhaps is not entirely far fetched. As calculations made here for the USSR are extended to other socialist countries, it may be hoped that we shall have a better basis than we now have to judge this intriguing question.

Industrial Productivity

I have been considering productivity in the economy generally, apart from diverse service branches. How does productivity in the Soviet Union compare with that in the West in nonfarm branches alone?

The question is in order, the more so when we consider that productivity in the economy generally is affected by productive efficiency not only within agriculture but in respect of the allocation of resources between that and other sectors. As we saw, that allocation is apt to be historically conditioned, and hence only partly determined by prevailing economic working arrangements. By comparing productivity in nonfarm branches, we are able to observe performance apart from such historical conditioning. While performance within the important agricultural sector is also excluded, our inquiry is usefully extended to embrace a comparison of nonfarm productivity in the countries studied.

Selected service branches again being omitted, the nonfarm branches in question include manufacturing, mining, power, construction, transport and communications, and trade. I shall refer to all these sectors together as "industry," though industry is thus construed in a relatively broad sense. As before, I have calculated output per worker and per composite unit of labor and capital. Reference is to the gross output originating in the branches in question.

With the comparison so delineated, the United States apparently is still preeminent among Western countries (Table 5). Other Western countries, however, are affected variously. Britain performs no better and perhaps somewhat worse relative to the United States than it did before. Germany, France, and Italy, however, all gain on the United States, the gain being greater for France than for Germany, and still greater for Italy than for France.

These are not very surprising results. Productivity in industry, it might be supposed, would tend to be higher than that in agriculture and perhaps the more so the greater the importance of agriculture in the economy. That must be so where, for historical reasons, employment in agriculture is inordinately large. With industrial productivity supplanting productivity in the economy generally as the yardstick, a country's performance relative to that of the United States should improve more or less commensurately with the comparative share of the excluded agricultural sector in its economy and in that of the United

TABLE 5
GROSS INDUSTRIAL PRODUCT PER EMPLOYED WORKER AND PER UNIT OF FACTOR INPUTS, SELECTED COUNTRIES, 1960[a]
(USA = 100 percent)

	Gross industrial product per worker (1)	Gross industrial product per unit of factor (labor and reproducible capital) inputs (2)
United States	100	100
France	60	71
Germany	54	69
United Kingdom	48	61
Italy	46	60
USSR	50	58

a) Gross industrial product represents essentially the gross output originating in manufacturing, mining, power, construction, transport and communications, and trade. In the calculation of output per worker and per composite unit of factor inputs, reference is to employment and capital stock used in the same sectors. Valuation of output and inputs is as in Table 1. Employment is also adjusted for hours in the same way as in Table 1, For sources and methods see Appendix.

States. That is indeed the case, as may be seen at once by juxtaposing our results with the comparative data already set forth on the share of nonfarm sectors in total employment (Table 4).

These results obtain whether reference is to output per worker or to output per composite unit of labor and capital. As before, though, the latter yardstick is the more significant one for our purposes.

What of the USSR? Here too performance improves relative to that of the United States. As might be expected in view of the still very large share of agriculture in the Soviet economy, the gain is especially marked. In terms of industrial productivity, the USSR is now practically on a par with Italy and also with the United Kingdom. The United Kingdom, for the reasons just indicated, no longer enjoys any margin to speak of over Italy. The Soviet performance, however, is still somewhat less impressive in terms of factor than in terms of labor productivity.

As previously, productive efficiency may diverge from factor productivity because of differences in the educational and sex structure of the population, but if we allow for such differences rather crudely as we did before, we see that Western countries other than the United States gain on that country much as before (Table 6). So too does the USSR, but that country now appears somewhat to surpass Italy when output per worker is the yardstick. In terms of factor productivity, however, the USSR still only matches Italy. Here again the United Kingdom is only more or less on a par with Italy, so productivity in the USSR is comparable to that in the United Kingdom as well as Italy.

TABLE 6
GROSS INDUSTRIAL PRODUCT PER EMPLOYED WORKER AND PER UNIT OF FACTOR INPUTS, WITH EMPLOYMENT ADJUSTED FOR QUALITY, SELECTED COUNTRIES, 1960[a]
(USA = 100 percent)

	Gross industrial product per employed worker	Gross Industrial product per unit of factor (labor and reproducible capital) inputs
	(1)	(2)
United States	100	100
France	68	78
Germany	65	79
United Kingdom	53	66
Italy	56	70
USSR	61	68

a) Employment adjusted throughout for differences in education, and sex and age structure, as well as hours. See text. For sources and methods, see Appendix.

Productive efficiency may also diverge from factor productivity in industry due to causes other than differences in labor quality, but these are much the same as those making productive efficiency diverge from factor productivity in the economy generally. What I have said regarding the latter causes essentially applies here as well.

I conclude, therefore, that productive efficiency in industry probably varies among Western countries, though not as much as in the economy generally. As for the USSR, in respect to productive efficiency, that country compares more favorably with the West in industry than in the economy generally. Most likely, it still only matches the least efficient of the Western countries studied, but that now means not only Italy but the United Kingdom. Also, to repeat, the margin between the worst and the best Western performance has now narrowed.

What again of the stage of economic development? May not differences in that now as before be a source of observed variations in factor productivity among Western countries? If so, may they not account as well for the still relatively low factor productivity and hence productive efficiency in Soviet industry? By focusing on industry alone, we have excluded one important way in which the development stage might affect factor productivity, that is through an historically conditioned misallocation of resources between agriculture and industry. As we saw, however, factor productivity might vary with the development stage for other reasons, and these should still be operative.

Stage of development seems most properly gauged at this point, though, from the capital stock per worker in industry. Among Western countries factor productivity very possibly does vary broadly with the development stage, as so viewed (Table 7; Chart 3),[20] but, as before, the Soviet Union does not seem to fit in well with the Western pattern. Perhaps the low productivity there relative to that in the United States is partly explicable in terms of the less advanced develop-

TABLE 7
CAPITAL STOCK PER WORKER AND FACTOR PRODUCTIVITY IN INDUSTRY, SELECTED COUNTRIES, 1960[a]
(USA = 100 percent)

	Capital Stock per worker with labor		Factor productivity with labor	
	Unadjusted for quality (1)	Adjusted for quality (2)	Unadjusted for quality (3)	Adjusted for quality (4)
United States	100	100	100	100
France	49	55	71	78
Germany	37	45	69	79
United Kingdom	33	37	61	66
Italy	32	39	60	70
USSR	50	63	58	68

a) For capital stock per worker, reference is to reproducible fixed capital and, in both variants, to employment adjusted for differences in hours. On factor productivity, see Tables 5 and 6. For data on reproducible fixed capital stock per worker, see Appendix, Table A-2.

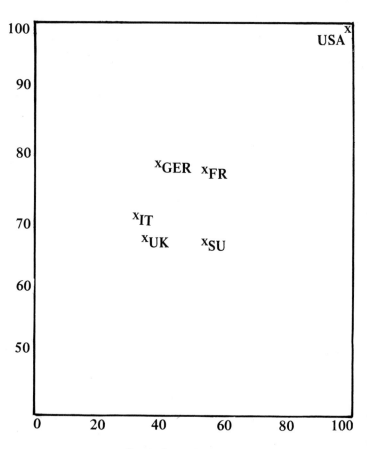

CHART 3.
*Capital Stock per Worker and
Factor Productivity in industry,
Selected Countries, 1960*

*Capital stock per worker
(USA = 100)*

ment of the Soviet Union, but by the same token that country now seems to compare less favorably with Italy and the United Kingdom than it did before. As previously, there is no assurance in any event that factor productivity varies with the development stage similarly under socialist central planning and capitalist mixed systems. What has been said of comparative factor productivity should hold as well for comparative productive efficiency.

Conclusions

I have sought in this essay to contribute to the appraisal of the comparative economic merit of socialism and capitalism. Attention has been focused on relative productive efficiency, as indicated by comparative labor and factor productivity, and on socialism, as represented by centralist planning in the Soviet Union, and capitalism, as represented by the variously mixed economies of the United States, France, Germany, the United Kingdom, and Italy.

This is a rather novel approach to comparative economic merit, and the inquiry perhaps has been justified if it merely demonstrates that the approach is also promising, and so should stimulate further research such as has been attempted. Additional research is in order to improve on the quality of the complex data required, and also to provide observations on comparative performance of countries other than those studied. Such additional observations are needed especially in judging how representative the countries studied regarding economic performance might be of countries with similar economic working arrangements.

Meantime, though, we may have succeeded in providing further evidence of how far socialism is economically from the system critics once held it would be, and also from the system that proponents have often envisaged. As found in the USSR, socialism is neither colossally wasteful, nor extraordinarily efficient, but well within those extremes, so familiar in polemics on socialist economic merit. Even so, however, productive efficiency in the USSR may well be low by Western standards. That may be so in industry as well as in the economy generally, including agriculture. As might be expected, though, industrial efficiency is greater than that of the economy generally, including agriculture.

Productive efficiency represents the degree to which total output corresponds to capacity. Closely related, though not the same thing, is the degree to which output structure conforms to prevailing preferences. Our comparative data on productivity may to some extent reflect performance in that respect as well as productive efficiency. But it should be observed that the Soviet performance regarding output structure by all accounts leaves much to be desired. That appears so from the standpoint of either "consumers' preferences" or any likely "planners' preferences." Extension of the appraisal fully to embrace performance regarding output structure, therefore, could not be very favorable to the USSR.[21]

The level of productivity of a country at any time may be viewed as representing the product of its level at any earlier date and its growth over the period thus delineated. Since available technological knowledge is normally increasing over time, the growth of productivity, even of the factor variety, does not indicate any corresponding increase in productive efficiency, as understood here, which relates simply to the effectiveness in use of whatever technological knowledge may be available. Among different countries that are economically interrelated, however, technological knowledge increases for all more or less to the same extent. Hence comparative trends in productivity may be more or less indicative of concomitant comparative trends in productive efficiency. It is of interest, therefore, that an extended comparison that has been made of productivity trends over time in not only the USSR but other countries of socialist centralist planning and also many capitalist mixed economies seems no more favorable to socialist centralist planning than the comparison made here.[22]

As the same study shows, given socialist centralist planning it has often been possible to compensate for any lag in the growth in productivity through the famous political control that is exercised over the rate of investment. Through a resultant rapid increase in the capital stock, a rapid increase in total output still has been achieved. Growth of output on that basis, however, has necessarily been costly to consumers, and, as each day's news reminds us, socialist governments have had to concern themselves increasingly lately with such costs. But comparative performance regarding growth, important as it is, is properly the subject of another inquiry. I must also leave for such inquiry extension of the appraisal in still other directions of interest. Needless to say, there are such, for comparative economic merit is indeed a many-faceted thing. It should help put that intricate matter in perspective, however, if even limited light has been shed here on comparative productive efficiency.

Technical Note[23]

I show in Table 8 selected data concerning various regression relations alluded to in the text. All the data pertain to relations of the form

$$Y = aX + bS + k$$
(1)

where Y represents factor productivity, X is an indicator of the stage of economic development, and S is a dummy variable standing for the presence or absence of socialism. All regression relations were calculated from six observations on the relations of the variables in question, either in the economy generally (Table 4) or in industry (Table 7).

Rows I A-C and II A-C all relate to the economy generally. In IA-C, reference is to regressions where Y represents factor productivity, with labor unadjusted for quality. The variable X represents, in I-A, the share of nonagricultural branches in total employment, in I-B, the capital stock per worker, and in I-C, the capital stock per worker, with labor adjusted for quality. In rows II A-C, all relations considered are as in I A-C, except

TABLE 8
Selected Data on Various Regressions

		Text Table	2ᵃ	a		b		k	
I	A	4	.59	1.146	(1.498)ᵇ	- .8706	(.03424)	-28.63	(.4415)
	B	4	.96	.6330	(6.875)	-17.81	(2.894)	37.29	(7.352)
	C	4	.94	.6937	(5.996)	-20.97	(3.039)	30.76	(4.537)
II	A	4	.56	.8780	(1.337)	- 3.140	(.1440)	.1429	(.0026)
	B	4	.94	.5123	(5.732)	-15.73	(2.633)	49.31	(10.02)
	C	4	.94	.5645	(5.488)	-18.26	(2.976)	43.86	(7.277)
III	A	7	.98	.5614	(11.29)	-14.09	(4.515)	44.02	(15.71)
	B	7	.99	.6210	(14.18)	-19.04	(7.561)	37.92	(14.45)
IV	A	7	.92	.4369	(5.401)	-10.51	(2.071)	56.67	(12.43)
	B	7	.94	.4893	(6.668)	-14.42	(3.417)	51.59	(11.74)

a) ρ^2 = coefficient of correlation
b) Parenthetic figures are t values. Each has the sign of the constant to which it refers.

that Y represents factor productivity with labor adjusted for quality.

Rows III A-B and IV A-B relate to industry. In III A-B, Y is factor productivity with labor unadjusted for quality. In III A, X is the capital stock per worker. In III-B, it is the capital stock per worker with labor adjusted for quality. In IV A-B, all is as in III A-B except that Y represents factor productivity with labor adjusted for quality.

Notes

* Research for this study was done partly with the aid of a grant from the National Science Foundation (Contract G-1525).

1. *Economics of Soviet Planning* (New Haven, Conn., 1964), pp. 340 ff; *Planning and Productivity under Soviet Socialism* (hereafter PPSS) (New York, 1968); "East-West Comparisons and Comparative Economic Systems: A Reply," *Soviet Studies* (October 1971); "Comparative Productivity and Efficiency in the Soviet Union and the United States" (hereafter *Productivity*), in Alexander Eckstein, ed., *Comparison of Economic Systems* (Berkeley, Calif., 1971). These studies all deal, at least in part, with the appraisal of comparative productive efficiency from comparative data on productivity. Sometimes, however, a further concern is to appraise from comaparative data on change in productivity over time relative "technological progress," including gains in

productive efficiency. I have also explored that problem in "National Income," in Abram Bergson and Simon Kuznets, eds., *Economic Trends in the Soviet Union* (Cambridge, Mass., 1963), and in "Development under Two Systems: Comparative Productivity Growth Since 1950," *World Politics* (July, 1971). Finally, mention perhaps should also be made of another related inquiry: "The Comparative National Income of the USSR and USA," in National Bureau of Economic Research, Conference on Research in Income and Wealth, *International Comparisons of Prices and Output* (New York, 1972).

2. *Why Growth Rates Differ* (Washington, D.C., 1967).

3. Housing apart, the services omitted here do not comprise all of the components of national income for which output is measured by factor inputs, but they generally represent the bulk of such sectors. Note that, from the present standpoint, the case for omission of such services is the greater since typically in national income accounting output of these services is measured by inputs of only one factor, labor. Inputs of reproducible capital and land typically are not represented at all.

As is proper, I exclude from gross material product only output originating in the service sectors in question. Output originating elsewhere but employed in the provision of services is still included. In the case of defense, for example, gross material product excludes the services of military personnel but includes munitions.

Output originating in housing is omitted along with output originating in the other services in question, but with the available data it was not feasible to exclude from the number of employed workers those engaged in providing housing services. The capital stock represented by housing, however, is of course omitted from that considered.

On the scope of national income according to the Soviet concept, see Abraham Becker, "National Income Accounting in the USSR," in V. G. Treml and J. P. Hardt, eds., *Soviet Economic Statistics* (Durham, N. C., 1972).

4. What if in each comparison of a foreign country with the United States, valuation were instead in terms of the prices of the foreign country? Regrettably it was not possible to make such calculations here, but from broadly similar computations made elsewhere, it seems safe to assume that, with substitution of foreign national for US dollar prices, the spread in productivity levels among Western countries would tend to widen. The USSR should be related to these countries, however, essentially as here. This is most clearly indicated for productivity in the economy generally, which is here in question, but most likely the same relations obtain for productivity in industry alone. I refer below to the latter. See *PPSS*, pp. 19ff; *Productivity*, pp. 178ff.

5. Denison, 1967, pp. 113-114.

6. To return to incentive arrangements, as the primers teach, these could conceivably induce too much effort as well as too little. On comparative incentive arrangements and effort generally, see *ibid.*, pp. 112ff., and *PPSS*, pp. 34ff.

7. See, however, the interesting information collated in Central Intelligence Agency, "Unemployment in the Soviet Union, Fact or Fiction?" ER 66-5 (March, 1966).

8. Tsentral'noe Statisticheskoe Upravlenie (hereafter, TSU), *Narodnoe khoziaistvo SSSR v 1960 godu* (Moscow ,1961), p. 646; Denison, 1967, p. 163.

9. On the possible importance of disparities in resource endowment as a cause of productivity differences

among the countries studied, see Denison, 1967, Ch. 14; *Productivity*, p. 192.

10. According to J. S. Bain, *International Differences in Industrial Structure* (New Haven, 1966), p. 65, among twenty US manufacturing industries studied, "the proportion of total industry output supplied by plants of reasonably efficient scale lay uniformly between 70 and 90 percent."

11. *Ibid.,* pp. 55ff., 144ff.

12. In Chart 1 reference is to factor productivity with labor adjusted for quality. In Chart 2, however, productivity as so determined is related to capital stock per worker with labor unadjusted for quality.

13. Among Western countries, the figure on capital stock per worker for the United Kingdom is surprisingly low. Perhaps it is too low, but it should be noted that I refer to the economy exclusive of selective services. In at least one service sector, housing, the British capital stock per worker turns out to be relatively high. See Denison, 1967, p. 129. As for the USSR, with all that is known about the high rate of capital investment maintained there through the years, one is still struck that the country compares as favorably with the West as our data show. There seems to be no reason to think the Soviet capital stock per worker is over-, rather than understated, but, to repeat, the data on capital stock per worker generally are crude.

As an indicator of the stage of economic development, capital stock per worker might be misleading here even apart from limitations in the data from which that relation is compiled. As is well known to the technically initiated, calculation of factor productivity requires aggregation of inputs of labor and capital with weights corresponding ideally to the shares of output properly imputable to the two factors. In practice, however, such ideal shares can at best be approximated. So far as the weights applied do diverge from them, as can readily be seen, the relation between factor productivity and capital stock per worker must to some extent be affected. In which direction the relation would be affected, though, would depend on the nature of the divergence. Thus, with too large a weight for capital, factor productivity should vary inversely rather than positively with capital stock per worker.

14. For the technically inclined, though, I should explain that in formulating the foregoing findings I have sought to take into account here various regression relations between factor productivity and indicators of the stage of economic development that are explained in the Technical Note. Later I will present some comparative data compiled for industry alone and will refer again in that context to the question of the relation of factor productivity to the stage of economic development. There too I take into account regression relations described in the Technical Note.

15. See Abram Bergson, *The Economics of Soviet Planning* (New Haven, Conn.), 1964, Ch. 11.

16. According to Denison, 1967, p. 292, "In the field I have termed 'technological knowledge,' a gap presumably exists, but I have difficulty in supposing that it is of any great importance." I wonder whether that is entirely realistic as to the rapidity of dissemination of new knowledge. For a case study that seems to corroborate Denison, however, see John E. Tilton, *International Diffusion of Technology: The Case of Semi-Conductors* (Washington, D.C. 1971).

Denison and Tilton refer, however, to Western countries. In the case of the USSR, as indicated, acquisition of new technological knowledge from abroad might take longer. It should also be observed, though, that in technologies actually in use the USSR may often lag behind the West for quite other reasons, particularly because the USSR may not be very prolific regarding new discoveries even for a country at its stage of development, and because of deficiencies in procedures for applying new knowledge already at hand. See *PPSS*, Ch. 3.

17. On the possible import of divergencies in economic working arrangements for differences in factor productivity among Western countries, see Denison, 1967, pp. 292ff.

18. The most important divergence by far is that represented by the shift from centralist planning to relatively decentralized systems, emphasizing markets, in Yugoslavia, beginning in the early fifties, and in Hungary in January, 1968. But from the standpoint of the stage of development, these two countries bracket a number of others where centralist planning is still practiced. In Czechoslovakia, one of the most advanced of all socialist countries today, a similar transformation was initiated in the mid-sixties, but apparently efforts to that end were much dampened by the events of August, 1968.

Among countries where centralist planning is still practiced, the presumption must be that, if only in degree of sophistication, procedures vary with the stage of development, but this intriguing question still remains to be explored.

19. I referred earlier to superiority of managerial practices as a possible reason for the high level of US productivity. Quality of managerial practices, however, is not easy to delineate from quality of managerial personnel. So far as managerial personnel is superior in the USA, the resultant gain in productivity would represent another instance of the kind of statistical deficiency in the measurement of the labor skill in question.

20. In the chart, factor productivity with labor adjusted for quality is related to capital stock per worker with labor unadjusted for quality.

21. As I explained, in compiling comparative data on productivity for Western countries, I use index numbers of output that are in terms of US factor cost. In order to relate Soviet to US productivity, however, I value output at US market prices. As the reader who is at all familiar with the technicalities will see, only the latter comparison should be especially affected by relative performance regarding output structure, but even so it can hardly reflect fully the proverbially inordinate amount of substandard and low quality goods produced in the USSR. See *Productivity*, p. 195, and Bergson, "The Comparative National Income of the Soviet Union and United States," pp. 153 ff.

22. Bergson, in *World Politics* (July, 1971). See also *PPSS*, Ch. 3.

23. I am indebted to Jonathan Eaton for assistance in carrying out the calculations summarized in this note.

APPENDIX:
SOURCES AND METHODS
ON COMPARATIVE PRODUCTIVITY

This appendix explains the sources and methods used in compiling the comparative data on output per worker and per composite unit of factor (labor plus reproducible capital) inputs in Tables 1, 2, 5, and 6 in the text. As will become clear, the calculations made are often crude. While they may, I think, still serve for the present purposes, care should be exercised in using them in other ways.

In Tables 1, 2, 5, and 6, reference is, on the one hand, to "gross material product" and to the factor inputs corresponding to that output and, on the other, to the gross product originating in "industry" and to the factor inputs corresponding to that output. As was indicated, "gross material product" is the gross output of the economy, excluding that originating in health care, education, public administration, defense, and housing. The gross product originating in "industry" is the gross material product, less output originating in agriculture. In each case, output is generally related to corresponding inputs, but employment throughout includes that in housing.

The comparative data on output per worker and per composite unit of factor inputs for the two spheres in question were compiled from the intercountry index numbers of employment, reproducible capital, and output in Tables A-1 and A-2. I first refer to these index numbers, and then to the weights employed in aggregating the index numbers for different factor inputs into corresponding measures of total factor inputs. The latter measures, of course, were needed for the calculation of output per composite unit of factor inputs.

Employment, unadjusted

The index numbers of employment, adjusted for hours, and those for employment, adjusted for hours, education, sex, and age, in Tables A-1 and A-2, are derived from the data in Table A-3 on employment prior to any adjustment. In the table agriculture includes and industry excludes forestry and fisheries, but I show parenthetically for the USA and USSR figures for agriculture exclusive, and for industry, inclusive of forestry and fisheries.

For Western countries, for *agriculture,* inclusive of forestry and fisheries, see Organization of Economic Cooperation and Development (hereafter OECD), *Labor Force Statistics, 1958-1969,* Paris, 1971. For the United States, employment in forestry and fisheries is taken to be .29 millions, as in US Department of Commerce, *The National Income and Product Accounts of the United States, 1926-1965* (hereafter, *US National Income, 1966*), Washington, D.C., 1966, pp. 112-113. Employment in *industry* is calculated as a residual.

Regarding *selected final services,* other than defense, for the United States employment in health care is the sum of employment in "medical and other health services, other than hospitals" and in "hospitals," in US Bureau of the Census, *Census of the Population, 1960,* Series PC(2)-7F, *Subject Reports: Industrial Characteristics,* Washington, D. C., 1967, p. 6. For education, I cite the sum of employment in "Public education" and "Educational services," in *US National Income, 1966,* pp. 112-113. For public administration, see OECD, *Statistics of the Occupational and Educational Structure of the Labor Force in 53 Countries,* Paris, 1969, p. 109. The Census figure cited

TABLE A-1
INDEX NUMBERS OF FACTOR INPUTS AND OUTPUT,
TOTAL ECONOMY (EXCLUSIVE OF SELECTED SERVICES),
SELECTED COUNTRIES, 1960
(USA = 100)

	Employment, adjusted for hours (1)	Employment, adjusted for hours, education, sex, and age (2)	Reproducible fixed capital (3)	Inventories (4)	Gross Material product (5)
United States	100.0	100.0	100.0	100.0	100.0
France	30.1	25.9	13.4	18.1	15.4
Germany	43.2	35.7	15.4	23.1	21.9
United Kingdom	40.2	36.5	14.1	24.6	19.8
Italy	33.8	26.2	8.6	13.7	11.4
USSR	162.5	120.1	54.6	77.9	50.5

TABLE A-2
INDEX NUMBERS OF FACTOR INPUTS AND OUTPUT, INDUSTRY, SELECTED COUNTRIES, 1960
(USA = 100)

	Employment, adjusted for hours (1)	Employment, adjusted for hours, education, sex, and age (2)	Reproducible fixed capital (3)	Inventories (4)	Gross product originating (5)
United States	100.0	100.0	100.0	100.0	100.0
France	24.7	21.9	12.1	16.5	14.8
Germany	40.6	33.8	15.1	24.0	22.1
United Kingdom	42.7	38.5	14.3	27.1	20.3
Italy	24.3	19.8	7.7	13.0	11.1
USSR	98.0	79.6	49.8	77.8	48.7

TABLE A-3
Employment by Sector, Selected Countries, 1960
(millions)

| | Agriculture | Industry | Selected final services | | | | | All |
			Health Care	Education	Public Administration	Defense	All	
	(1)	(2)	(3)	(4)	(5)	(6)	(7)	(8)
United States	5.46 (5.17)a	51.75 (52.04)a	2.59	3.32	2.66	2.51	11.08	68.29
France	4.19	12.04		2.48		.84	3.32	19.55
Germanyb	3.62	19.80	.59	.49	1.45	.29	2.82	26.24
United Kingdom	1.03	20.78		1.24	1.21	.52	2.97	24.78
Italy	6.52	11.87	.10	.65	.86	.37	1.98	20.37
USSR	(39.3)a	(49.0)a	3.5	5.0	2.0	3.3	13.8	102.1

a) Figures shown parenthetically relate to agriculture exclusive, and industry inclusive, of forestry and fisheries.
b) Including West Berlin.

there relates to April 1, 1960, and is here increased by .7 percent in order to obtain a figure centered on July 1, 1960.

For all selected final services, including defense, for France, I take as a point of departure data for 1950 calculated from various US-French occupation and branch per capita employment relatives for that year in Milton Gilbert and Irving B. Kravis, *An International Comparison of National Products and the Purchasing Power of Currencies*, Paris, n.d., pp. 39, 177, 180; and Milton Gilbert and Associates, *Comparative National Products and Price Levels*, Paris, n.d., p. 50. Corresponding absolute employment data for sectors of interest are obtained by reference to related occupational and branch employment data for the United States in 1950 in US Bureau of Census, *Census of Population 1950*, Series P-E, No. 1C, *Special Report, Occupation by Industries*, Washington, D. C., 1954, pp. 12, 68; *US National Income, 1966*, pp. 112-113; and OECD, *Statistics of Occupational and Educational Structure of the Labor Force in 53 Countries*, p. 104; OECD, *Manpower Statistics, 1950-1962*, Paris, 1963, p. 125. Reference is also made to the comparative population of France and the United States in 1950, as given in the OECD study above.

For all selected final services, including defense, employment in France is taken to increase by 45 percent from 1950 to 1960, chiefly in the light of data on the concomitant change in gross product originating in "public administration" (including public health care and education) and defense, and on the comparative magnitude of that and the gross product originating in private health care and education in OECD, *Statistics of National Accounts, 1950-1961,* Paris, n.d., p. 91. Finally, employment in final services other than defense is calculated by reference to the OECD figure on employment in defense in 1960 to which I refer below.

For employment in selected final services other than defense in Germany, see OECD, *Statistics of the Occupational and Educational Structure of the Labor Force in 53 Countries,* p. 38. Figures given for 1961 are extrapolated to 1960 in the light of annual data on civilian employment in OECD, *Labor Force Statistics, 1958-1969,* p. 97. Also, the cited figure for employment in education in 1961, .6 million, is reduced to .5 million in order to exclude employment in scientific research institutes.

For the United Kingdom, employment in health care, education, and public administration is calculated for 1950 by use of the same sources and methods as were used in calculating employment in all final services in France in that year. For health care and education, employment is taken to increase from 1950 to 1960 by 17.8 per-

cent, in the light of data on the gross product
originating in public health care and education,
in current prices, and implied price trends for
miscellaneous services, in OECD, *Statistics of
National Accounts, 1950-1961*, p. 197. Employment in public administration, in 1950, together
with defense in that year, as given in OECD,
Manpower Statistics, 1950-1962, p. 115, is taken
to decline by 1960 by 5.2 percent, in the light
of data on real gross product originating in public administration and defense. See OECD, *Statistics of National Accounts, 1950-1961*, p. 197.
From the resulting figure for employment in public administration and defense in 1960, I deduct
employment in defense in 1960, as explained
below.

In Italy, employment in selected final services other than defense in 1950 is estimated,
sometimes not very reliably, by use of essentially
the same sources and methods as were used to
calculate such employment in 1950 for France.
I extrapolate health care and education to 1960
by reference to data on trends in employment of
teachers in OECD, *The Mediterranean Regional
Project, Italy*, Paris 1965, p. 44. Public administration employment is extrapolated similarly by
reference to data on employment in the "civil
service," *ibid.*, p. 29.

For employment in *defense* in all Western

countries, see OECD, *Labor Force Satistics, 1958-1969*. Employment in *all sectors* is from the same source.

Employment by sector in the USSR is from *Productivity*, p. 203, except that employment in education, given there as 5.7 million, is reduced here to 5.0 million in order to make it more nearly comparable in scope to employment in education in Western countries. Particularly, the concern is to limit the coverage of employment in scientific research institutions, and in branches such as entertainment. The figure of 5.0 million is nevertheless derived on the supposition that employment in education in the USSR and USA is proportional to the number of teachers and scientific workers in the two countries, as determined chiefly from data in TSU, *Narodnoe khoziaistvo SSSR v 1960 godu*, Moscow, 1961, p. 34, and the US Bureau of the Census, *Census of Population, 1960*, Series PC(2)-7C, *Subject Reports: Occupation by Industry*, Washington, D. C., 1963, pp. 7-8.

Employment, adjusted for hours

Elements in the adjustment of employment for hours are shown in Table A-4. To refer first to Western European indices relative to the USA, for columns (1) and (2), see Table A-3. Note that "all sectors" here comprises "agriculture" and "industry" in the latter table. For purposes of deriving columns (3) and (4), I take comparative hours for agricultural and industrial workers in the countries considered in 1960 to correspond to those for agricultural and nonagricultural workers in those countries in an autumn week in 1960 in Denison, 1967, p. 55. Resulting indices with US industrial hours as 100 percent are then corrected to allow for differences in vacation time and in loss of time due to weather in the observed week. See Denison, 1967, pp. 363ff. The indices are also adjusted on the supposition that hours in excess of those worked by US industrial workers in 1960 are properly discounted, the discount to vary with the excess according to a scale in Denison, 1967, pp. 58ff. Column (4) follows at once. So too does column (3), after the adjusted indices for agriculture and industry are averaged with appropriate employment weights (Table A-3), and a shift is made in the base, so that the US average for the two spheres is 100 percent.

In columns (5) and (6), the resulting indices are further adjusted to allow for the fact that, for purposes of productivity calculations, such coefficients are properly applied only in industries where output is not measured by inputs. I take into account data in Denison, 1967, p. 188, on the share of labor inputs in civilian activities

TABLE A-4

Adjustment of Employment for Hours, All Sectors (Exclusive of Selected Final Services) and Industry, Selected Western Countries, 1960

(USA = 100)

	Employment, unadjusted		Hours worked, adjusted		Hours worked, further adjusted		Employment adjusted	
	All sectors	Industry	All sectors	Industry	All sectors	Industry	All sectors [(1)x(5)]	Industry [(2)x(6)]
	(1)	(2)	(3)	(4)	(5)	(6)	(7)	(8)
United States	100.0	100.0	100.0	100.0	100.0	100.0	100.0	100.0
France	28.4	23.3	106.4	106.5	105.9	105.8	30.1	24.7
Germany	40.9	38.3	106.0	106.5	105.6	106.0	43.2	40.6
United Kingdom	38.1	40.2	105.9	106.8	105.4	106.2	40.2	42.7
Italy	32.1	22.9	106.3	108.0	105.3	106.0	33.8	24.3
USSR	154.3	94.2	195.3	104.0	105.3	104.0	162.5	98.0

for which output is measured by employment. Such labor inputs occur to a great extent in selected final services, which are in any event omitted from both the output and inputs of concern here. Allowance need be made now only for labor inputs such as are in question additional to those in selected final services, as indicated in Table A-3.

Turning to the indices for the USSR in Table A-4, for columns (1) and (2) see Table A-3. To explain columns (3) and (4) reference is made to Table A-5. To begin with columns (1) and (2), in the United States workers in agriculture and in nonfarm branches, taken here to represent industry, averaged 45.5 and 40.0 hours weekly during 1960. Reference is to averages calculated from monthly data in US Department of Labor, *Monthly Report on the Labor Force*, January-December, 1960. The corresponding annual totals of 2366 and 2080 hours are reduced by 3.7 and 6.5 percent in order to allow for eight holidays and also, somewhat arbitrarily, for vacations. See Denison, 1967, p. 363, and data on vacation time in the US Department of Labor report just cited.

For the USSR, agricultural workers are taken to work eight hours a day for an average 280 day year. See US Bureau of the Census, *International Population Reports*, Series P-91, No. 15, *Estimates and Projections of the Labor Force and Civilian Employment in the USSR, 1950-1975*, Washing-

TABLE A-5

Elements in Calculation of Coefficients for Hours, All Sectors
(Exclusive of Selected Final Services) and Industry, USA and USSR, 1960

	Annual hours		Annual hours (US industry = 100)		Annual hours, adjusted (US industry = 100)	
	Agri-culture	Industry	Agri-culture	Industry	Agri-culture	Industry
	(1)	(2)	(3)	(4)	(5)	(6)
United States	2278	1945	117.1	100.0	109.1	100.0
USSR	2240	2057	115.2	105.8	108.7	104.0

ton, D. C., June, 1967, p. 19; Nancy Nimitz, *Farm Employment in the Soviet Union, 1928-1963,* RAND RM-4623PR, Santa Monica, November, 1965, pp. 10, 11, 123. At the end of 1960, workers in nonfarm branches, which I take to represent industry, were employed an average of 39.4 hours weekly. See TSU, *Narodnoe Khoziaistvo SSSR v 1960 godu,* p. 645. This reflects reductions of working time during 1960. For 1960 as a whole, hours were on the average an estimated 6.3 percent higher than at the end of 1960, or 41.9 weekly. I rely here chiefly on data in Central Intelligence Agency, *An Evaluation of the Program for Reducing the Work Week in the USSR,* ER 61-13, March, 1971. The implied annual total, 2179 hours, also reflects holidays and shorter hours before free days and holidays, but not, I believe, vacations, averaging in 1960 17.4 working days, or at 7 hours a day, 122 hours: TSU, *Narodnoe knoziaistvo v 1968 godu,* Moscow, 1969, p. 207. Net of vacations, therefore, industrial workers averaged 2057 hours in 1960.

The indices in columns (3) and (4) follow and so too do those in columns (5) and (6) after hours in excess of those of US industrial workers are discounted here in the same way as in the calculation of Western European coefficients.

To return to the Soviet coefficients in Table A-4, that for industry in column (4) corresponds to that for industry in Table A-5, column (6).

The coefficient for all sectors in Table A-4, column (3), is calculated by averaging, with appropriate employment weights (Table A-3), the coefficients for agriculture and industry in Table A-5, columns (5) and (6). In Table A-4, in the case of Soviet coefficients, no further adjustment is made to allow for labor inputs in activities where output is measured by employment. Such activities beyond those in excluded services are believed to be relatively limited in the case of the USSR.

In adjusting employment for hours worked, I make no allowance for loss of time due to sickness. Such an allowance is made for Western countries in Denison, 1967, p. 364, but it evidently had to be rather conjectural, and it seemed best to omit it here for all countries alike. Because of generous arrangements for pregnancy leave, time lost due to sickness is appreciable in the USSR; in industry, it averaged 16.6 days in 1960. See TSU, *Narodnoe Khoziaistvo v SSSR v 1968 godu*, p. 207. In terms of a seven-hour work day, that comes to 116 hours or 5.6 percent of the nonfarm work year. In the circumstances, omission of any allowance for time lost due to sickness probably is somewhat disadvantageous to the USSR. That seems more clearly so, however, when that country is compared with the United States than when it is compared with Western Europe. It is also more clearly so in the comparison of productivity in industry than in that in all sectors.

While Soviet hours should thus sometimes be relatively overstated, it should be noted that there is also something of a bias to the contrary so far as the USSR, as distinct from other countries considered, reference here is to normal hours exclusive of overtime.

Employment, adjusted for hours, education, age and sex

Elements in this calculation are shown in Table A-6. For column (1), see Table A-4. Column (4) is simply the product of columns (2) and (3), except that for Western European indices an allowance is made as before for labor inputs in activities for which output is measured by employment, or rather for such activities beyond those represented by selected final services. Column (5) is obtained as indicated in the table. It remains to explain Table A-6, columns (2) and (3).

To refer first to column (2), the indices there follow from Table A-7, columns (3) and (4). Turning to that table, and to begin with to the

TABLE A-6

ADJUSTMENT OF EMPLOYMENT FOR EDUCATION, SEX AND AGE, ALL SECTORS (EXCLUSIVE OF SELECTED FINAL SERVICES), AND INDUSTRY, SELECTED COUNTRIES, 1960

(USA = 100)

	Employment adjusted for hours (1)	Educational quality (2)	Quality as affected by sex and age (3)	Quality as affected by education, sex and age, adjusted (4)	Employment adjusted for hours, education, sex and age [(1)x(4)] (5)
			All Sectors		
United States	100.0	100.0	100.0	100.0	100.0
France	30.1	86.8	97.8	86.1	25.9
Germany	43.2	85.8	94.8	82.6	35.7
United Kingdom	40.2	91.7	98.2	90.9	36.5
Italy	33.8	74.9	97.6	77.4	26.2
USSR	162.5	81.0	91.2	73.9	120.1

TABLE A-6 (CONT.)

	Employment adjusted for hours (1)	Educational quality (2)	Quality as affected by sex and age (3)	Quality as affected by education, sex and age, adjusted (4)	Employment adjusted for hours, education, sex and age [(1)x(4)] (5)
			Industry		
United States	100.0	100.0	100.0	100.0	100.0
France	24.7	89.3	97.8	88.7	21.9
Germany	40.6	86.3	94.8	83.3	33.8
United Kingdom	42.7	90.8	98.2	90.2	38.5
Italy	24.3	77.1	97.6	81.5	19.8
USSR	98.0	86.7	93.6	81.2	79.6

TABLE A-7
INDICES OF EDUCATIONAL QUALTIY OF EMPLOYMENT, BY SECTOR, SELECTED COUNTRIES, 1960

(US eighth grade quality = 100)

	All sectors including selected final services (1)	Agriculture (2)	Industry (3)	All sectors excluding selected final services (4)
United States	118.9	103.0	120.3	118.7
France	103.6	90.3	107.4	103.0
Germany	102.0	90.8	103.8	101.8
United Kingdom	108.8	100.1	109.2	108.8
Italy	89.2	81.9	92.7	88.9
USSR	97.3	85.5	104.3	96.2

indices there for Western countries, for column (1) for the United States see Denison, 1967, p. 91. For other Western countries, corresponding figures are obtained essentially by applying to the US figure indices, with the United States as 100, of educational quality based on school years completed in Denison, 1967, p. 91. The latter indices were obtained by Denison, however, on the assumption that the armed forces are educationally equivalent everywhere and also after an adjustment for the length of the school year. I reverse the latter adjustment and also abandon Denison's assumption regarding the armed forces, though the indices thus obtained are treated as relating to civilian workers. The necessary revisions of Denison's indices are made on the basis of data in Denison, 1967, pp. 87, 91-92.

The indices in columns (2) and (3) represent the results of an attempt to disaggregate between farm and nonfarm workers the indices in column (1). The indices thus obtained for nonfarm workers are taken here to apply also to industrial workers alone. The disaggregation takes into account coefficients of educational quality as related to years of schooling in Denison, 1967, p. 374 (his Table F-2, column [4]), and diverse distributions of the labor force by years of schooling.

For the United States I refer particularly to such distributions for male and female farm workers in 1960 in US Bureau of the Census, *US Census of Population, 1960,* Series PC(2)-7F, *Industrial Characteristics,* pp. 98, 100. I first aggregate these distributions, counting one female farm worker as .63 of a male farm worker (see below), and then calculate from the combined distribution and the Denison coefficients of educational quality as related to years of schooling an index of average educational quality for farm workers in 1960. A corresponding index for nonfarm workers is calculated as a residual.

For France, Germany, and the United Kingdom, I refer to data relating to various dates on the distribution of male and female workers in all sectors by years of schooling in Denison, 1967, pp. 385, 390, 396. I first aggregate the separate distributions for the two sexes, using as weights shares of the two sexes in the wage bill at US wage rates. See Denison, 1967, p. 87. I then disaggregate the resultant distribution between farm and nonfarm workers on the rather arbitrary assumption, but I think one not seriously amiss here, that farm workers had completed no more than seven (in England, eight) years of schooling, and that they were distributed by years of schooling up to that level in the same way as workers in all sectors. Indices of average educational quality for farm and nonfarm workers obtained on this basis for various dates are shifted to 1960 by reference to the relation between the implied index for workers in all sectors and the corresponding index in column (1).

For Italy, I refer to a distribution of male workers alone in all sectors by years of schooling in Denison, p. 80, but the rest of the indices for that country in columns (2) and (3) are obtained in the same way as those for other Western European countries.

To complete the discussion of indices for Western countries in Table A-7 those in column (4) are obtained by averaging with appropriate employment weights (Table A-3) the indices in columns (2) and (3).

Turning to the USSR, indices of educational quality for all workers and for nonfarm workers are derived as explained in *Productivity*, pp. 205-206. The index for nonfarm workers thus obtained is taken here too to apply to industrial workers, while a corresponding index for farm workers is calculated as a residual. In doing so, I apply to the different coefficients in question appropriate employment weights (Table A-3), though a female worker is counted as equal to only .68 of a male worker. On this discount and on the breakdown thus needed of employment in different sectors by sex, see below. Finally, by use of similar employment weights, I average the indices thus derived for agricultural and industrial workers in order to obtain the single index in column (4) for the two spheres together.

In Table A-6, for column (3) for Western European countries, I take indices in Denison, 1967, p. 75, for civilian workers generally to apply also to such workers, excluding those in selected final services, and to industrial workers alone. For the USSR, the corresponding indices are calculated from indices of US hourly earnings by sex and age in Denison, 1967, p. 72, and data on the distribution of employment by sector, sex, and age in the USA and USSR in Table A-3;

Denison, 1967, p. 72; US Bureau of Labor Statistics, *Employment and Unemployment Statistics, 1947-1961*, Washington, D. C., October, 1962, p. 10; and TSU, *Itogi vsesoiuznoi perepici naseleniia 1959 goda SSSR*, Moscow, 1967, pp. 117ff. I also refer to data on employment by sector and sex in *Productivity*, p. 203, though in somewhat revised form to conform to Table A-3.

Reproducible fixed capital; inventories

For Western countries, the indices for reproducible fixed capital stocks for all sectors, excluding selected services, in Table A-1 are obtained as averages of indices of "enterprise" nonresidential reproducible fixed capital stocks, gross and net of depreciation, in Denison, 1967, p. 172. Corresponding indices for industry alone in Table A-2 are calculated by reference to the share of agriculture in the reproducible fixed, nonresidential "business" capital of the United States in 1960, taken to be 9.0 percent. See the data on constant cost 2 capital stocks based on straight line depreciation in R. C. Wasson, J. C. Musgrave, and Claudia Harkins, "Alternate Estimates of Fixed Business Capital in the United States, 1925-1968," *Survey of Current Business*, April, 1970, p. 30.

Relative to the reproducible fixed capital stock in agriculture in the United States, I assume that the stock in each of the other Western countries considered corresponds to the farm output of that country compared to that in the United States. Comparative farm output in different Western countries is obtained as explained below. The indicated assumption is arbitrary, but the resulting indices of agricultural capital conform fairly well to alternative indices derived from the indices for all sectors, excluding selected final services, and data on the share of agriculture in gross fixed investment between 1950 and 1960, in OECD, *Statistics of National Accounts, 1950-1961*. This is shown in the accompanying table.

REPRODUCIBLE FIXED CAPITAL
IN AGRICULTURE (USA = 100),
CALCULATED BY REFERENCE TO

	Output	Gross Investment, 1950-60
United States	100.0	100.0
France	27.1	17.3
Germany	18.6	16.7
United Kingdom	11.0	9.1
Italy	17.6	18.6

Note that for France, gross investment data were available only for 1956 to 1959. Also, even a sizable error at this point would hardly affect results of interest. Thus, if the French index for agricultural fixed capital were 17.3, instead of 27.1, as assumed, the corresponding index for industry would be 13.0 instead of 12.1. Factor productivity in industry in France would be 69.8 instead of 70.8 percent of that in the United States.

For the USSR, the indices of reproducible fixed capital in Tables A-1 and A-2 also represent averages of indices of such capital, gross and net of depreciation. As for the latter indices these are calculated from data on the reproducible fixed capital stocks of the USSR and USA on July 1, 1960, in US dollar prices of 1955. For the USSR, see *Productivity*, p. 208. For the United States, corresponding data are derived from the figures on constant cost 2 capital stocks, based on straight line depreciation, in Wasson, Musgrave, and Harkins, *Survey of Current Business*, April, 1970, p. 30. Data on capital stocks in 1958 dollars in this source are translated to US dollars of 1955 by reference to deflators supplied by the Office of Business Economics, US Department of Commerce. To make the results comparable with my data on Soviet capital stocks, I add to the resulting totals US highway capital, as given in *Productivity*, p. 209.

For Western countries, the indices for inventories in all sectors, excluding selected final services, in Table A-1, are those on "enterprise" inventories in Denison, 1967, p. 177. (Here and elsewhere inventories in agriculture include livestock herds.) Corresponding indices for industry alone, in Table A-2, are obtained by reference to the share of agriculture in such inventories in the United States, taken to be 15.2 percent. See *Productivity*, p. 209. As with reproducible fixed capital, I assume that, relative to farm inventories in the United States, those in other Western countries vary in proportion to farm output. For the indices for inventories in the USSR, see *Productivity*, p. 209.

Output

In Tables A-1 and A-2, indices of Western European gross material product and gross product originating in industry are calculated from Table A-8. In that table, for the *gross domestic product* of the United States, see OECD, *National Accounts of OECD Countries, 1958-1967*, Paris, n.d., p. 44. Corresponding figures for the other countries are derived from the cited figure for the United States, indices of Western European relative to US net national product in US factor cost in Denison, 1967, p. 22, and comparative data on net national product and gross domestic prod-

TABLE A-8

GROSS DOMESTIC PRODUCT BY SECTOR, SELECTED WESTERN COUNTRIES, 1960, IN US FACTOR COST OF 1960

(billions of dollars)

	United States (1)	France (2)	Germany (3)	United Kingdom (4)	Italy (5)
Agriculture	21.0	5.7	3.9	2.3	3.7
Industry	355.7	52.5	78.6	72.3	39.4
Selected final services					
Health care	13.6	⎤	3.4	⎤	.5
Education	14.9	⎬ 11.9	2.2	⎬ 5.1	2.9
Public administration	14.6	⎦	8.0	6.6	4.7
Defense	10.6	3.5	1.2	2.2	1.6
Housing	33.4	3.9	6.1	6.6	1.9
All	87.1	19.3	20.9	20.5	11.6
All sectors	463.8	77.5	103.4	95.1	54.7

uct at factor cost in national currencies in the OECD report just cited.

In Table A-8, *agriculture* includes forestry and fisheries. For the gross domestic product of the United States originating in that sector in US market prices, see the cited OECD report. To convert to US factor cost, I allow for indirect business taxes and government payments to land-lords, as given in *US National Income*, 1966, p. 29.

FARM OUTPUT

France	222.1
Germany	155.2
Italy	125.8

For the United Kingdom, I take the gross product originating in agriculture to be 10.9 percent of that for the United States. I refer here to comparative data for the UK and USA for the gross product originating in agriculture in 1950 in US prices of that year, in Deborah Paige and Gottfried Bombach, *A Comparison of National Output and Productivity*, Paris, 1959, p. 19, and to data for the UK and USA on the gross product originating in agriculture, forestry and fisheries in 1950 and 1960, in constant prices, in OECD, *Statistics of National Accounts, 1950-1961*.

For other Western European countries, farm

output in 1960 varied as is indicated in the accompanying table relative to that of the United Kingdom as 100 percent. Reference is to gross farm output, less farm products used in production, in average Western European prices, as supplied to me by the Food and Agricultural Organization, United Nations (hereafter, FAO), in a letter of August 30, 1971. In Table A-8, the gross domestic product originating in agriculture in France, Germany, and Italy is calculated from these indices, after their adjustment to exclude production expenses in other than farm products. The latter are estimated from data in FAO, *Expenses and Income of Agriculture in Some European Countries*, Geneva, 1958.

For all countries, the gross domestic product originating in *industry* is calculated as a residual. Turning to *selected final services*, for the United States the gross domestic product originating in health care is obtained as the product of employment there (Table A-3) and the corresponding average earnings including "supplements," as estimated from data in Central Intelligence Agency, *A Comparison of Consumption in the USSR and the US*, ER 64-1S, January, 1964, p. 83; and *US National Income, 1966*, pp. 96-97, 108-109, 114-115. For education, reference is to labor earnings in "Educational Services" and "Public Education," as determined from the data given in *US National Income, 1966*, pp. 92-93, 96-97, 114-115.

For public administration, I cite the product of employment there (Table A-3) and average labor earnings, including "supplements," for an essentially comparable sector, as calculated chiefly from data in *US National Income, 1966,* pp. 69, 92-93, 112-113, 114-115, together with Table A-3, and the calculations just made for health care and education. For defense, see *US National Income, 1966,* p. 69.

The gross domestic product originating in housing is taken to be 7.2 percent of the gross domestic product at factor cost, or the same proportion as it is of the gross domestic product at market price. See OECD, *National Accounts of OECD Countries,* 1958-67, p. 46.

Turning to selected final services for Western European countries, product originating in health care, education, and public administration is extrapolated from data on such output in 1950 in US prices of 1950. The latter data are calculated from per capita quantity relatives (USA = 100) in Gilbert and Kravis, n.d., pp. 113-119, 177, 180, comparative population data in OECD, *Manpower Statistics, 1950-1962,* and data on the product originating in the services in question in the United States in 1950, as determined by use of essentially the same sources and methods as were used to derive such data for the United States in 1960 in Table A-8. For health care in Italy, I take the per capita product originating in 1950 to be

15 percent of that in the United States. This seems rather low, though in Gilbert and Kravis, p. 177, in per capita terms all health care outlays (for personnel and materials) in Italy in 1950 are taken to be but 10 percent of those of the United States.

In extrapolating the 1950 product to 1960 and translating to US prices of 1950, I refer to trends in employment and in US prices in the sectors in question as determined from calculations already made in connection with Table A-3 and use sources and methods essentially such as were employed in those calculations. Elements in the foregoing derivation of product originating in health care, education, and public administration are set forth in Table A-9.

For defense, I cite for all Western European countries the product of the size of the armed forces (Table A-3) and the average pay and subsistence of military personnel in the United States, $4225 per year. See US National Income, 1966, pp. 69, 112-113.

For housing, product originating in Western European countries is calculated from that originating in the United States (Table A-8) and corresponding Western European quantity relatives (USA = 100). The latter relatives are extrapolated from such relatives for 1950, that are derived from per capita quantity relatives for final outlays ("space rent" only) for housing in Gilbert

and Kravis, n.d., pp. 113-119, 135-136. In extrapolating to 1960, I refer to changes in the gross
domestic product originating in "ownership of
dwellings," in constant prices, for Western European countries, in OECD, *Statistics of National
Accounts, 1950-1961,* and OECD, *National Accounts of OECD Countries, 1958-1967;* and in
personal outlays on "housing" in constant prices
in the United States, in *US National Income,
1966,* pp. 48-49.

In Tables A-1 and A-2, indices of Soviet gross
material product and of Soviet gross product
originating in industry are calculated from Table
A-10. Here agriculture excludes, and industry includes, forestry and fisheries. For the United
States, the gross national product and the gross
product originating in agriculture in 1960, in 1955
dollars, are given in *Productivity,* p. 200. I trans-
late these outputs in terms of 1960 dollars by
reference to deflators in OECD, *Statistics of National Accounts, 1950-1961,* pp. 209-210. The
gross product of industry is calculated as a residual. For selective final services other than
housing, see Table A-8. For housing, see OECD,
*National Accounts of OECD Countries, 1958-
1967,* p. 46.

For the USSR, gross national product by sector in 1960 in US prices of 1955 is as in *Productivity,* p. 198 except that farm output is reduced
to 16.4 billion dollars in order to conform to cal-

TABLE A-9
Calculation of Product Originating in Health Care, Education, and Public Administration, Selected Western European Countries, 1960

	Outlays, 1950, in US Prices of 1950 (USA = 100)	Outlays, 1950, in US Prices of 1950 (billion dollars)	Employment Relative, 1960÷1950 (percent)	Outlays, 1960, in US Prices of 1950 (billion dollars) [(2)x(3)]	US Price Relative 1960÷1950 (percent)	Outlays, 1960, in US Prices of 1960 (billion dollars) [(4)x(5)]
	(1)	(2)	(3)	(4)	(5)	(6)
France						
Health care	17.9	.95				
Education	21.8	1.20				
Public administration	32.8	2.23				
All		4.38	1.62	7.10	167.3	11.88
Germany						
Health care	29.9	1.58	1.37	2.16	159.6	3.45
Education	15.4	.85	1.48	1.26	176.4	2.22
Public administration	43.5	2.96	1.61	4.77	167.9	8.01
All		5.39				13.68

TABLE A-9 (CONT.)

	Outlays, 1950, in US Prices of 1950 (USA = 100) (1)	Outlays, 1950, in US Prices of 1950 (billion dollars) (2)	Employment Relative, 1960÷1950 (percent) (3)	Outlays, 1960, in US Prices of 1950 (billion dollars) [(2)x(3)] (4)	US Price Relative 1960÷1950 (percent) (5)	Outlays, 1960, in US Prices of 1960 (billion dollars) [(4)x(5)] (6)
United Kingdom						
Health care	24.0	1.27				
Education	23.7	1.30	1.18	3.03	168.4	5.10
Public administration	54.4	3.70	1.07	3.96	167.9	6.65
All		6.27				11.75
Italy						
Health care	4.6	.24	1.36	.33	159.6	.53
Education	22.2	1.22	1.36	1.66	176.4	2.93
Public administration	36.5	2.48	1.13	2.80	167.9	4.70
All		3.94				8.16

TABLE A-10
GROSS NATIONAL PRODUCT BY SECTOR, USA AND USSR, IN 1960, IN US MARKET PRICES OF 1960
(Billions of dollars)

	United States (1)	USSR (2)
Agriculture	20.5	17.4
Industry	391.5	190.8
Selected final services		
Health care	13.6	18.4
Education	14.9	22.4
Public administration	14.6	11.0
Defense	10.6	13.9
Housing	36.5	7.5
All	90.2	73.2
All sectors	502.2	281.4

culations in Abram Bergson, "Comparative National Income of the USSR and USA," in National Bureau of Economic Research, Conference on Research in Income and Wealth, *International Comparison of Prices and Output,* New York, 1972.

Also, industrial output is once again calculated as a residual, and these data, all in billions of dollars, are now used for selected final services: health care, 14.66; education, 17.03; public administration, 8.37; defense, 11.11, and housing, 6.9. For each of these sectors except housing, I cite the product of employment in the sector in 1960 (Table A-3) and the corresponding earnings, including "supplements" in the United States in 1955, as determined from Central Intelligence Agency, *A Comparison of Consumption in the USSR and the US*, p. 83; *US National Income, 1966*, pp. 69, 96, 112, 114-115. In 1955 dollars, housing output in 1960 is taken to be 20.5 percent of that of the US. See *Productivity*, pp. 198, 200. US housing output in 1960 in 1955 dollars is calculated from such output in 1960 in 1960 dollars (Table A-10), and implied deflators for housing in *US National Income, 1966*, pp. 162-163.

Gross output originating in agriculture in 1960 in 1960 dollars is calculated from that output in 1955 dollars by reference to the deflator applied above in the corresponding translation for the United States. Gross output originating in industry in 1960 in 1960 dollars is calculated from that output in 1955 dollars on the assumption that the corresponding prices rose 10.5 percent from 1955 to 1960. This is the deflator implied by comparative data on gross industrial output of the United States in 1960 and 1955 dollars. For that output in 1960 dollars, see Table A-10. The corresponding figure for gross industrial output in 1955 dollars, 354.3 billion, represents a revision of the figure, 343.7 billion dollars, for such output in 1955 dollars in *Productivity*, p. 200. The revision takes account of changes in estimates for selective final services implied by diverse calculations in this appendix.

In dollars of 1960, selected final services, other than housing, in the USSR in 1960 are calculated by reference to comparative Soviet and US employment in 1960 in the sectors in question (Table A-3) and the gross product originating in those sectors in the United States in 1960 (Table A-10). For housing, output in 1960 in 1955 dollars is translated into such output in 1960 dollars by application of the implied deflators for housing in *US National Income, 1966*, pp. 162-163. Gross national product in 1960 in 1960 dollars is obtained as the sum of the foregoing components.

Factor input weights

In calculating factor productivity, I aggregate factor inputs with weights corresponding to their shares in US gross output in 1960, as given in Table A-11. In the United States in 1960, *labor income* for all sectors, including selected final services, is estimated to have been 324.5 billion dollars. This is the sum of compensation of employees, 294.2 billions, as given in *US National Income, 1966*, pp. 14-15, and the labor income of proprietors, 30.3 billion, as estimated from data

TABLE A-11
FACTOR INCOME SHARES, USA, 1960

	All sectors excluding selected final services		Industry	
	Billion Dollars (1)	Percent (2)	Billion Dollars (3)	Percent (4)
Labor	270.8	74.15	260.1	75.37
Reproducible fixed capital				
Net	45.7		41.6	
Depreciation	37.5		33.9	
Gross	83.2	22.78	75.5	21.88
Inventories	11.2	3.07	9.5	2.75
All	365.2	100.00	345.1	100.00

in *U.S. National Income, 1966*, pp. 22-23. I assume that 80 percent of all proprietors' income is labor income, including compensation of employees. See *U.S. National Income, 1966*, pp. 22-23 and Denison, 1967, p. 37. Labor income in all sectors, excluding selected final services, is obtained by deducting labor earnings in selected final services. See Table A-8. In order to obtain labor income in industry, I also deduct labor income in agriculture. This is 10.7 billion dollars, or the sum of compensation of farm employees, 2.8 billions, as given in *US National Income, 1966*, p. 93, and labor income of farm proprietors, taken to be 7.9 billion dollars or 66 percent of all proprietors' income, the same share as labor income of proprietors is found above to constitute of proprietors' income in all sectors. On proprietors' income in agriculture, see *U.S. National Income, 1966*, pp. 14-15.

All *nonlabor income* in all sectors, including selected final services, but net of depreciation, is calculated to be 90.0 billion dollars. This is the difference between national income, 414.5 billions, given in *U.S. National Income, 1966*, pp. 14-15, and labor income as determined above. Corresponding earnings of reproducible fixed capital and inventories in sectors other than selected final services are calculated by applying to all nonlabor income in all sectors the percentage shares of such income imputed to nonresidential structures and equipment and inventories, in 1960 to 1962, in Denison, 1967, p. 38. Earnings from reproducible fixed capital and inventories in industry are taken to be respectively 91.1 and 84.8 percent of such earnings in the economy generally, exclusive of selected final services. I refer to the shares of industry in the reproducible fixed capital and inventories of the economy generally, exclusive of selected final services, as calculated from the US Department of Commerce data on US business fixed capital referred to above and from data on inventories in *Productivity*.

Depreciation on reproducible fixed capital in the economy generally, exclusive of selected final services, corresponds to that on business fixed capital in the Commerce Department constant cost 2 calculations based on straight line depreciation. Similarly for industry I refer to such depreciation for business fixed capital other than that in agriculture. The pertinent figures were supplied by the US Department of Commerce, Office of Business Economics.

Abbreviations

FAO: Food and Agricultural Organization

OECD: Organization for Economic Co-operation and Development

PPSS: Abram Bergson, *Planning and Productivity under Soviet Socialism*

Productivity: Abram, Bergson, "Comparative Productivity and Efficiency in the Soviet Union and the United States"

TSU: Tsentral'noe Statisticheskoe Upravlenie

US National Income, 1966: US Department of Commerce, *The National Income and Product Accounts of the United States, 1926-1965*

Bibliography

Bain, J. S. *International Differences in Industrial Structure,* New Haven, 1966.

Becker, Abraham. "National Income Accounting in the USSR," in V. G. Treml and J. P. Hardt, eds., *Soviet Economic Statistics,* Durham, N. C., 1972.

Bergson, Abram. "National Income," in Abram Bergson and Simon Kuznets, eds., *Economic Trends in the Soviet Union,* Cambridge, Mass., 1963.

———. *Economics of Soviet Planning,* New Haven, Conn., 1964.

———. *Planning and Productivity under Soviet Socialism,* New York, 1968.

149

————. "Development under Two Systems: Comparative Productivity Growth Since 1950," *World Politics* (July, 1971).

————. "East-West Comparisons and Comparative Economic Systems: A Reply," *Soviet Studies* (October, 1971).

————. "Comparative Productivity and Efficiency in the Soviet Union and the United States," in Alexander Eckstein, ed., *Comparison of Economic Systems*, Berkeley, California, 1971.

————. "The Comparative National Income of the USSR and USA," in National Bureau of Economic Research, Conference on Research in Income and Wealth, *International Comparisons of Prices and Output*, New York, 1972.

Central Intelligence Agency. *A Comparison of Consumption in the USSR and the US*, ER 64-1S, January, 1964.

————. *An Evaluation of the Program for Reducing the Work Week in the USSR*, ER 61-13, March, 1971.

————. *Unemployment in the Soviet Union, Fact or Fiction?*, ER 66-5, March, 1966.

Denison, Edward F. *Why Growth Rates Differ*, Washington, D. C., 1967.

FAO. *Expenses and Income of Agriculture in Some European Countries*, Geneva, 1958.

Gilbert, Milton and Associates. *Comparative National Products and Price Levels,* Paris, n.d.

Gilbert, Milton and Irving B. Kravis. *An International Comparison of National Products and the Purchasing Power of Currencies,* Paris, n.d.

Nimitz, Nancy. *Farm Employment in the Soviet Union, 1928-1963,* RAND RM-4623PR, Santa Monica, November, 1965.

OECD. *Labor Force Statistics, 1958-1969,* Paris, 1971.

——. *Manpower Statistics, 1950-1962,* Paris, 1963.

——. *The Mediterranean Regional Project, Italy,* Paris, 1965.

——. *National Accounts of OECD Countries, 1958-1967,* Paris, n.d.

——. *Statistics of National Accounts, 1950-1961,* Paris, n.d.

——. *Statistics of the Occupational and Educational Structure of the Labor Force in 53 Countries,* Paris, 1969.

Paige, Deborah and Gottfried Bombach. *A Comparison of National Output and Productivity,* Paris, 1959.

Tilton, John E. *International Diffusion of Technology:* The Case of Semi-Conductors, Washington, D. C., 1971.

TSU. *Narodnoe khoziaistvo SSSR v 1960 godu,* Moscow, 1961.

————. *Itogi vsesoiuznoi perepici naseleniia 1959 goda SSSR*, Moscow, 1967.

————. *Narodnoe knoziaistvo v 1968 godu*, Moscow, 1969.

US Bureau of Census. *Census of Population 1950*, Series P-E, No. 1C, *Special Report, Occupation by Industries*, Washington, D. C., 1954.

————. *Census of Population, 1960*, Series PC(2)-7C, *Subject Reports: Occupation by Industry*, Washington, D. C., 1963.

————. *Census of the Population, 1960*, Series PC(2)-7F, *Subject Reports: Industrial Characteristics*, Washington, D. C., 1967.

————. *International Population Reports*, Series P-91, No. 15, *Estimates and Projections of the Labor Force and Civilian Employment in the USSR, 1950-1975*, Washington, D. C., June, 1967.

US Department of Commerce. *The National Income and Product Accounts of the United States, 1926-1965*, Washington, D. C., 1966.

US Bureau of Labor Statistics. *Employment and Unemployment Statistics, 1947-1961*, Washington, D. C., October, 1962.

US Department of Labor. *Monthly Report on the Labor Force*, January-December, 1960.

Wasson, R. C., J. C. Musgrave and Claudia Harkins. "Alternate Estimates of Fixed Business Capital in the United States, 1925-1968," *Survey of Current Business* (April, 1970).

THE BEST SOCIETY:
EFFICIENCY AND EQUALITY

Fritz Machlup

In hundreds of years of argument for and against socialism the two most heatedly argued claims have been that a socialist economic system would be superior to a capitalist or a mixed economy in (1) *productive efficiency* and (2) *distributive justice*.

The first claim is very clearly put in the formulation proposed in Professor Bergson's paper: that the working arrangements of a socialist system are instrumental in achieving greater productive efficiency, reflecting a better utilization of the potential productivity of labor and capital. Bergson has tested this proposition and finds that empirical evidence shows precisely the opposite. The second claim identifies distributive justice with equality of income. This is the theme of Professor Tinbergen's paper.

Bergson's paper presents a comparison of productive efficiency in Soviet Russia with that in four Western countries. Tinbergen's paper contains no comparison of the degree of inequality of personal incomes or consumption in Soviet Russia and in our mixed economies. Instead, it offers arguments in favor of institutions designed to equalize personal incomes anywhere, in socialist, capitalist, and mixed economies, indeed in the whole world.

I conceive my task to be chiefly that of a critical commentator. Since I have little time but much criticism of Tinbergen's paper, I shall indulge unashamedly in a grossly unequal distribution of my time and give almost all that I have left to Tinbergen.

Tinbergen complains about the common practice of "welfare economists to keep the ethical contribution out as long as possible and only have it brought in after the economic analysis had been finished." He recommends that the required "ethical choice be made at the beginning." Ethical choices can be made only on the basis of postulates, and postulates cannot be judged to be true or false. At best, they can only be judged as commanding or not commanding common assent. In support of a postulate one may offer a persuasive "prod to acceptance" but never a "proof." This has been said by many writers, but I chose to quote it from a very fine article by the economist Robert Strotz. The title of that article was "How Income Ought To Be Distributed," and the subtitle was "A Paradox in Distributive Ethics."[1] A critical reply carried the subtitle "Paradox Lost,"[2] and the subtitle of Strotz's rejoinder was "Paradox Regained."[3] This afternoon we are again playing with the Perplexing Paradox of Paradise Presumed.

Tinbergen holds that "our attitude toward others [our fellow men] should be governed slightly only by envy. In other words: that solidarity feelings about cancel feelings of envy." I wonder whether the second sentence is supposed to be a normative statement, a prod, or a factual judgment about people's actual attitudes or preferences. I shall argue presently that it is false if it is meant to be a statement of fact, and pietistic if it is to be a moral precept. I recall the dictum of Oliver Wendell Holmes, Justice on the Supreme Court: "I have no respect for the passion for equality, which seems to me merely idealizing envy."[4] Well, I do have respect for idealists, but I agree that sheer envy and sympathetic envy (or second-order envy) are at the core of the ideal of income equality. John Stuart Mill called envy "the most anti-social and evil of all passions,"[5] and Friedrich Hayek warned against sanctioning the demands of envy "by camouflaging it as social justice."[6]

I do not believe that all or most proponents

of equality of income or consumption are motivated by self-interested envy. Instead, it is vicarious or reflected envy, one of the several forms of sympathy, that moves some men of affluence to reject their actually or potentially high standard of living and propose equal sharing with their fellow men. Tinbergen is an idealist in two respects: not only does he champion the ideal of equality of income distribution, but he also believes that the ideal of equal sharing is actually a top-priority objective of our society. He is not averse to letting governments impose certain rules and institutions on an unwilling people "if the population is shortsighted." In general, however, he wants to rely on public actions that maximize social welfare as indicated by "the social welfare function." From among several alternatives, he chooses "to take the sum of individual welfare values, without weights attached," as the valid social welfare function.

In this choice Tinbergen is not very far apart from several other writers on welfare economics. Kenneth Arrow, for example, speaks of the "aggregation of the multiplicity of individual preference scales." [7] But Tinbergen differs from most other writers in that he believes that the "welfare feelings" of individuals can be measured, compared, and aggregated (not only conceptually but actually) and in that he draws political conclusions from his (thus far only hypothetical) calculations. I admit, of course, that most people with less than average income probably favor equality of income, chiefly because they stand to gain by a redistribution at the expense of those better off. The beneficiaries of such a redistribution—though they would probably benefit only in the short run —would undoubtedly be in the majority.

Tinbergen offers five subtle distinctions in the "approaches" to the optimization of the social welfare function, depending on different assumptions about the integrability of individual welfare functions, about weights attached to them, and about the basic equality of people with regard to "sensitivity to the values" (to feelings) of pleassure and pain) and with regard to their capabilities and their needs (as to working conditions as well as consumption). One set of assumptions "would require equal incomes for everybody"; another, which Tinbergen regards as "more realistic," would require "that incomes should be equal after correction for differences in needs, both professional [like a personal library and study for Tinbergen or for me] and purely human needs."

Tinbergen is consistent in proposing redistribution from the rich to the poor not only "within each nation" but also "between nations," or "even more so, since primary (or productive) income inequality is much larger between than within nations." We might try to find out how our fellow citizens feel about sharing their wealth and income with the people living in the rest of the world. We could easily ask them, perhaps through survey research or in a referendum. A first, more general question, like "Are you in favor of greater equality of income among all the people of the world?" might get majority support. A more specific question, I am afraid, would be voted down overwhelmingly. It might be worded like this: "Would you favor a worldwide redistribution of income, with the result that the average income per person in the United States would be reduced from the present 4000 dollars (or so) to the world average of less than 400 dollars per person?" As a matter of fact, we may take the voting record of the U. S. Congress as an indication of the majority opinion of our citizens. Despite some urging by the President, Congress could not be persuaded to appropriate as much as one half of one percent of our national income for aid to poor countries. For the kind of sharing that would be needed to approach international equalization of income per head, the appropriation of the United States would have to be in the neighborhood of 90 percent of our national income.

I realize, of course, that for the description of a "world community welfare function" we must aggregate the individual welfare functions of all

the people of the world, and not confine our-
selves to the welfare functions of the American
people. In a worldwide referendum I would ex-
pect a majority to vote for radical redistribution,
so that the poor can share the wealth with the rich
—with the result that all would be equally poor.
The idea is that the welfare loss of the 200 million Americans, whose incomes are to be cut
down by 90 percent on the average, would be
smaller than the welfare gain accruing to the billions of people whose incomes would double or
quadruple from 100 or 200 to 400 dollars a year,
and that thereby world community welfare would
be raised and perhaps maximized.

An argument like this presupposes the possibility of interpersonal comparisons and measurement of utility or welfare. It presupposes that rob-
bing Peter to pay Paul would reduce Peter's
measurable happiness by x units and increase
Paul's $x + y$ units, with a combined net gain of y
units of happiness. Tinbergen, in his own words,
has the "tremendous optimism" necessary to make
the assumption that we shall be able to measure,
add, and subtract the "welfare feelings" of different people; that we shall have a good "welfare
thermometer" [or, as I would call it, a *hedom-
eter*]. But even if I shared this optimism, which
I do not, I would not be willing to conclude that
the expectation of an increase in their combined

162 THE BEST SOCIETY: EFFICIENCY AND EQUALITY

happiness implies a moral justification, let alone an ethical mandate, that we actually rob Peter to pay Paul.

Tinbergen no doubt realizes that the confiscation of excess incomes (the portion above the average) would affect people's efforts and exertions and that national and world incomes would fall as a result. This is why he wants to replace taxes on actual incomes by taxes on potential incomes. If people with greater capabilities were taxed on the incomes they *could* earn by working hard, they would have to work even harder if they wanted to keep an extra buck for themselves. Their earnings potentials would be assessed by comprehensive examinations—and Tinbergen thinks we will soon perfect our testing techniques to measure capabilities. He does not tell us about the simultaneous perfection of the cheating techniques of those examined. Surely, if we were taxed on high test scores, we should try hard to get low scores; we could then earn a little more than our tax assessment if we later performed beyond our tested and taxed capabilities. Alas, Tinbergen wants to have us retested every five or ten years and it might be a bit embarrassing to make a poor showing at the reexamination if we had by hard work outperformed our previous, poor test scores.

The test-and-tax game would, I suppose, work like this. If Tinbergen can solve ten differential equations in the time I need to solve one, he would have to pay a high tax to equalize our earning capacities, provided we live on this kind of work. If we live on our earnings from writing books and I can write two while he writes one, I would have to pay the higher taxes. It is not clear to me how testable capabilities to perform particular intellectual and manual tasks can be translated into earning capacities if earnings depend on the market prices of things produced, and prices, in turn, depend on demand. The earnings capacity of an opera singer does not depend merely on the number of high C's he can produce per week but also on the demand for opera performances. And how can one test the earnings capacities of managerial personnel, say, in banking, in industry, in commerce, in opera houses, and in universities? I wonder whether Tinbergen has given serious thought to his optimum tax scheme or whether he has offered it only as an interesting conversation piece.

The probable effects of income equalization upon workers' efforts and performance have been a major concern of the party chiefs in socialist countries. Let me quote from an early pronouncement of Joseph Stalin: "In order to insure our enterprises the necessary manpower, it is essential to attract the workers to the enterprises, so as to turn them into a more or less constant force. . . . Fluctuation of labor power has become a scourge to production. . . . It is due to incorrect organization of the system of wages, to an incorrect wage scale, to a leftist leveling of wages. . . . Leveling results in that the unskilled worker has no interest to become skilled. . . . Marx and Lenin say that the difference between skilled and unskilled labor will exist even under socialism, even after the abolition of classes, that only under communism will this difference disappear, because even under socialism 'wages' would be paid according to work done and not according to one's needs." [8]

This is only one example of the official party line. The leaders of the Communist parties in the socialist countries recognize that the incentive effects of differences in incomes are indispensable for productive efficiency in the socialist economy. With this reference to productive efficiency I have come back full circle to Bergson. I should have liked to give him at least a few morsels of criticism. I might at least have referred to him as the author of several classical studies on welfare economics and on the ideal of an optimization of the social welfare function.[9] Alas, the justice of giving equal time to the critique of two eminent scholars had to be sacrificed to the greater efficiency of distributing scarce time according to the marginal productivity of its competing uses.

Notes

1. Robert H. Strotz, "How Income Ought To Be Distributed: A Paradox in Distributive Ethics," *Journal of Political Economy*, Vol. LXVI (June 1958).

2. Franklin M. Fisher and Jerome Rothenberg, "How Income Ought To Be Distributed: Paradox Lost," *Journal of Political Economy*, Vol. LXIX (April 1961).

3. Robert H. Strotz, "How Income Ought To Be Distributed: Paradox Regained," *Journal of Political Economy*, Vol. LXIX (June 1961).

4. *The Holmes-Laski Letters: The Correspondence of Mr. Justice Holmes and Harold J. Laski, 1916-1935* (Cambridge: Harvard University Press, 1953), Vol. II, p. 942.

5. John Stuart Mill, *On Liberty* (first ed. 1859; Oxford: Oxford University Press, 1946), p. 70.

6. F. A. Hayek, *The Constitution of Liberty* (Chicago: University of Chicago Press, 1960), p. 93.

7. Kenneth J. Arrow, "Public and Private Values," in Sidney Hook, ed., *Human Values and Economic Policy* (New York: New York University Press, 1967), p. 13.

8. Joseph V. Stalin, *The New Russian Policy* (New York: John Day Company, 1931), pp. 6-8.

9. Abram Bergson, "A Reformulation of Certain Aspects of Welfare Economics, *Quarterly Journal of Economics*, Vol. LII (1938), pp. 310-334; "On the Concept of Social Welfare," *Quarterly Journal of Economics*, Vol. LXIII (1954), pp. 233-252.

SOCIAL ASPIRATIONS
AND OPTIMALITY

Oskar Morgenstern

If coming in alphabetical sequence is ever unfavorable, here you have an instance. Professor Machlup has stolen most of my thunder, so I will have to rely on a few remarks which involve more the technical aspects of the underlying questions which have been raised by our two distinguished speakers. I shall start with Professor Bergson who has given a most interesting discussion of a very complicated situation. He has shown a healthy skepticism with regard to the validity of the data with which he has to operate. But I feel that in the gradual development of his argument he has placed more and more reliance on exactly those facts which he has classified as rather doubtful at the beginning.

In addition to this, there is a question which I think is of singular importance. There has been

an emphasis on "productivity," but productivity
has been described essentially for physical output
and physical processes. But if you compare various countries, at present, or the same country, say,
the United States, over a long period of time, you
discover that in some countries physical output is
still very important, while in others, as in the
United States now, about 60 percent of the total
national income is generated by activities in
which physical output is a most unfathomable
and intangible entity. Services predominate rather
than physical output, and the notion of productivity in regard to service industries is one of the
weakest concepts in economics and thus should
be used in this particular connection only with
greatest restraint.

So I find there is a considerable difference
here in the general outlook. It is also not clear to
me to what extent, for example, management has
a role in explaining the differences which he has
shown to be of significant character for the United
States and in other countries, particularly the
Soviet Union.

In general, therefore, I find that Professor
Bergson has touched a very difficult area, which
it is very desirable to do. We are clearly not in the
comfortable situation as one is in the physical sci-
ences or at least in parts of it, but even there, for
example, Einstein has observed that most people
seem to think it is pretty clear what one should

observe and how one should observe it. Here we are in an area in which this issue must be raised, since the notion of productivity is still subject to so many great doubts.

Let me turn to Professor Tinbergen, with whom, as was the case for Professor Machlup, the differences go deeper than with Professor Bergson. A discussant, I think, has of course the duty to show where he differs rather than where he agrees. Now the first point is to say that behind everything that Professor Tinbergen described there lie extremely difficult abstract questions.

For example, the notion of an "optimum" seems to be a very clear concept, but it is far from it. To describe what an optimum is requires a very precise statement, if possible, in a mathematical and even axiomatic form, and I have seen nothing of this kind in Professor Tinbergen's discussion and no evidence that it is based on such investigations. He has taken optimum as something that is intuitively immediate and clear. But one has made many studies lately in economic theory from which it has resulted that it is not too difficult to show situations for which it can be proved that an optimum, however specifically defined, just does not exist.

That result then is in the nature of a counter-example. It works, as for example, in regard to those people who say all swans are white, and you show them a black swan, and thus the general statement is false. Therefore to talk about the existence of an optimum without proving that the particular optimum actually exists is a very questionable matter.

The next point is that there is an attempt in all these efforts to formalize society. But once more, I think it has also been shown lately that it is in principle impossible to formalize society. The attempts of this nature immediately run afoul of some principle or of some other opinion and the choice between opinion and these attempts of formalization becomes a very major issue.

Next, the fundamental equality of man is again a very dubious matter. In fact, I notice, that some, as Professor Tinbergen, get the Nobel prize, which doesn't make them exactly equal to the rest of us, and therefore if we were to equalize, we must impose changes which may cause great displeasure to some. The great, actual differentiation of incomes in socialist countries, to which Professor Machlup also referred, was driven home to me last year when I happened to be in Leningrad and was taken by a distinguished Russian scientist through the streets, and I pointed out various apartment houses, and asked who lives in this type of building and who lives in that type of building, and he said: "I cannot even begin to explain to you the differentiation that exists in the

Soviet Union among classes of people." And that in a country to which these studies have referred!

Another point of great importance is the following: Suppose we were to equalize incomes, how stable is the situation? What will hold equal incomes really equal in the long run? Would it not be necessary to interfere constantly if there should be tendencies to reestablish inequalities which, we think, are the consequence of the gifts people have regarding their capability to create incomes for themselves, which is, indeed, a great gift? There are differences among gifts of the kind possessed by great mathematicians, by great singers, by great artists—and by many others. Are there interferences needed and which would be required in order to attain the goal of equal incomes—acceptable to us? Would it not require imposition of some sort of dictatorship? Who determines whether equality should be maintained and even be attempted to be established?

It has also been shown that on the same physical background, one can establish various social organizations, each one having its own inner stability but all of them differing among each other. Choices from among these different alternative organizations, posed on the same physical background, become impossible without the introduction of views which are outside the particular system. That means, in this case, that views which are of an ethical, moral, or political character are called for. There is no scientific reason why one system should be preferred over the other. I do not think that it is as simple to resolve this issue by the devices which Profesor Tinbergen proposed at the beginning of his talk: namely, simply to postulate a particular value system which we should use, all of us, without any mechanism shown as to how this common agreement could be reached in a free society.

Society's preferences must be stated. We would certainly want to exclude dictatorship. There must be a process of free creation of systems of social preferences, and they will, I believe, certainly not lead to the idea of an equal distribution of incomes as a stable system, and we cannot prove the workability of such a hypothetical system scientifically by a long shot.

To summarize, I would say one is reminded of an idea which is very old and goes back to Nicholas Cusanus, that what is wanted is to adjust our inner thoughts and wishes to an ever better understood world in which we live. And that is to say, we must have aspirations and develop aspirations which are possible.

What we do in the physical world depends on our growing knowledge of physical phenomena. This determines the bounds of our activities. But where are the bounds of the social world in which we want to live? They do not only depend on our knowledge but also on our values and preferences and these differ over time and from country to country. Whatever emerges, I do not think it will be the world, at least in my view, in which Professor Tinbergen wants to live.